BED AND BREAKFAST
IN CALIFORNIA

"Picturesque lodgings are visible in all 400 entries in this enlarged guide. . . . Strong provides helpful tips, traveler's checklist, bed & breakfast association names, and an index."
—*Books of the Southwest*

". . . Visitors to California who wish to partake of nontraditional accommodations will find it a comprehensive and valuable guide."
—*The Midwest Book Review*

". . . The first comprehensive guide to such inns in the state."
—*Times-Press Recorder*, San Luis Obispo County, California

BED AND BREAKFAST
IN CALIFORNIA
Third Edition

by
Kathy Strong

A Voyager Book

The Globe Pequot Press

Chester, Connecticut

Illustrations in this book have been reproduced from establishments' brochures or literature, with the permission of the establishment. Special credit is given to the following artists, individuals or agencies.: The Ryan House, Helen Kendall; River Rock Inn, Carol Mathis; White Sulphur Springs Ranch, Janet Gogue; Golden Ore House Bed & Breakfast, Dan Schilling; Petersen Village Inn, Richard Yaco; Eastlake Inn, Ed Alejandre; Bluebelle House, Ann Serra; Heritage Park Bed & Breakfast Inn, Tillie Morse/Sun Graphics; La Mer, Sara Fine; Red Rose Inn, Charles Newman; Donnymac Irish Inn, Joe Romano; Ten Inverness Way, Jacquetta Nisbet; The Cobblestone Inn, Nancy Taylor; The Darling House, Daniel R. Dicicco; Culver's, Carol Beniott; Camellia Inn, Sonoma County Atlas of 1877; The Hope-Merrill & Hope-Bosworth Houses, Steve Doty; Beazley House, Mandy Fisher; The Plough and The Stars Country Inn, Patricia Bason; Agate Cove Inn, Sally Yost; Philo Pottery Inn, Brian McFann; The Grey Whale Inn, Bob Avery; Big River Lodge—The Stanford Inn, Larry Eifert; Joshua Grindle Inn, Dick Smith; Elk Cove Inn, Judith Brown; The Victorian on Lytton, Susan Elwart-Hall; Almond View Inn, Tom Morton; Christmas House Bed & Breakfast Inn, Bill Baldwin; B. G. Ranch and Inn, Marsha Mello; Chalet de France, Lili Vieyra; The Raford House, Robert Matson; Heritage Inn, The Publicity Mill; The Lemon Tree Inn, Wendell Dowling; The Little Inn on the Bay, Bob Bates.

Library of Congress Cataloging-in-Publication Data

Strong, Kathy, 1950–
    Bed & breakfast in California / Kathy Strong.
      p.   cm.
    "A Voyager book."
    Rev. ed. of: The California bed & breakfast book. c1986.
    Includes index.
    ISBN 0-87106-794-3 (pbk.)
    1. Bed and breakfast accommodations—California—Guide-books.
2. California—Description and travel—1981— —Guide-books.
I. Title. II. Title: Bed and breakfast in California.
TX907.S767 1988
647'.9479403—dc19   87-34219
                                                           CIP

Cover photo: Sean Kernan
Cover design: Barbara Marks

Manufactured in the United States of America
Third Edition/First Printing

*With special appreciation to the innkeepers
for their assistance and good wishes,
may your winter Mondays all be "full."*

About the Author

Also the author of the popular *Bed & Breakfast in the Caribbean* (formerly *The Caribbean Bed & Breakfast Book*), Ms. Strong, along with husband Rob, created and ran a nine-guestroom, turn-of-the-century b&b inn in Central California. Ms. Strong originally began work on this publication at the request of inn guests who were constantly inquiring about a book that would include descriptions of all the state's offerings. This third, thoroughly updated, and greatly expanded edition of *Bed & Breakfast in California* (formerly *The California Bed & Breakfast Book*) follows highly successful previous editions and offers more than four hundred bed & breakfast establishments throughout California and nearly twice as many attractive illustrations. Kathy hopes the book will not only better serve the experienced b&b fans but convince the timid first-timers to give this delightful kind of accommodation a try.

CONTENTS

CONTENTS

INTRODUCTION

This third edition of *Bed & Breakfast in California* (formerly *The California Bed & Breakfast Book*) is a must for any avid b&b traveler or for those who are considering sampling this exciting and personal way of touring the state. This thoroughly updated edition includes new information on inns listed previously plus entries on more than sixty new establishments—more than 400 in all! You will also find almost twice as many attractive illustrations to help you choose your perfect bed & breakfast. The new b&b listings include many interesting and historical landmark structures, gracious mansion estates, mountain-top chalets, quaint cottages, ocean-side villas, and Cape Cod charmers, to name just a few.

Bed & Breakfast in California invites you to venture out of your predictable and perhaps dull traveling routine and discover this gracious world of individuality, comfort, and warmth where you can indulge your dreams of opulence for a day or step back in history to relive days gone by. Sounds like a large promise? You'll find it isn't once you've ventured into the "unknown," for the underlying message in *Bed & Breakfast in California*, whether you're discovering a gold-rush hotel, a picturesque Victorian house, or a glass-enclosed suite overhanging the Pacific, is the certainty of a highly personalized and comfortable stay. After all, in this rapid-paced, computerized life nearly everyone is searching for a world that moves more slowly and relates more personally.

Bed & Breakfast in California encourages you to experience these overnight adventures, as varied and vast as the California scenery. If you've already sampled bed & breakfast travel here, you're undoubtedly yearning for more, for it's an exciting discovery that gives a whole new dimension to touring the "sunshine" state. Although bed & breakfast is hardly new (it was born and is practiced widely in Europe, is synonymous with New England America, and is more than twenty years old in California), it is just gaining momentum and high popularity in the West. And, as always, California has its own unique qualities to lend and blend with the old, established traditions known to bed & breakfast travel. That's where *Bed & Breakfast in California* shines as the adventure it truly is.

If bed & breakfast travel is such a glorious and fulfilling experience, then why, you may ask, is it currently enjoyed by only a small (be it rapidly growing) portion of the traveling community?

INTRODUCTION

One explanation is that the majority of bed & breakfast establishments in the state are still in their infancy, having mushroomed about countryside and cityside in the last few years faster than almost anyone can keep up with. The second reason is ironic yet true. Bed & breakfast travel is so varied in California that many travelers are timid about pioneering into this unknown territory, which seemingly lacks uniformity in any respect. If you are one of these reluctant but curious pioneers *Bed & Breakfast in California* will help you to become a courageous explorer discovering those special places in and about California's alluring valleys, peaks, deserts, and coastlines, reserving confidently and arriving enthusiastic about the very differences you are about to find. The following pages will guide the most cautious of you through the sometimes confusing and overwhelming aspects of what to expect, what to ask, and what to watch for, culminating with a detailed *Bed & Breakfast in California* "Traveler's Checklist" for especially easy reference.

The "Bed & Breakfast Directory" herein contains more than four hundred California b&b establishments and is the largest, most up-to-date directory available. A simple key with each b&b listing offers basic information about that particular establishment to help you narrow your search in any specific geographic area. But *Bed & Breakfast in California* highly recommends that you personally contact each establishment you are considering and request a brochure and/or additional information. It is the aim of *Bed & Breakfast in California* to present you with the most complete guide to b&b travel rather than be selective for you. A routine b&b to one may be a fantasy come true to another! You'll also notice blank entries at the end of each section so that you may enter new listings as you hear of them. The descriptions of the bed & breakfasts in this book are as accurate as possible. Sometimes, however, situations and/or owners change, and if you should find any of the accommodations not measuring up to your expectations, the author would very much appreciate your letting her know. However, most bed & breakfast travelers find that, once they know what to expect, disappointments are rare.

So, venture out into one of California's few remaining frontiers. The experiences you will have are sure to add spice and spirit to your travel and, above all, restore your belief that personal comforts, individuality, and hospitality are still part of California living.

PART ONE

EXPLORING CALIFORNIA
BED & BREAKFASTS

THE VARIETY OF CALIFORNIA'S
BED & BREAKFAST ESTABLISHMENTS

Drawing from Europe's popular and quaint pension, enterprising and always-innovative Californians have produced a bounty of that intimate and hospitable form of lodging in almost every imaginable size, style of architecture and furnishings, and location. In other words, you name it, and California bed and breakfast has it (or will very soon!). To give you an idea of the creative bed & breakfasts awaiting you, let's explore a sampling.

Size and Type

The size of bed & breakfast establishments ranges from the large inn, with as many as fifty rooms, to the small private home, with one or two rooms. Some of the inns contain amenities associated with hotels, and, indeed, some were at one time traditional hotels or boarding houses. Within these you may find restaurants, pools, spas, large lounges, and other hotel-type offerings. Smaller homes make up the majority of bed & breakfast establishments in the state and were, for the most part, single-family homes originally. Each of the inns is operated primarily as a bed & breakfast business with more businesslike hours, staffing, policies, and routine in general than is usually found in a private-home situation.

A cottage or guest house may be found in conjunction with an inn or may be an overnight rental all by itself in back of a private home. This separate dwelling inherently provides more privacy, often is more family-oriented, and sometimes offers cooking facilities.

Although a problem—local zoning regulations discouraging bed & breakfast use in residential areas—is on the rise, private homes offering from one to four bed & breakfast accommodations still exist in large numbers around the state. A few private homes with guest rooms are listed in the Directory, primarily those that remain independent from referral agencies. But the bulk of home listings can be found by contacting one of the several agencies also listed in this book who specialize in finding you bed & breakfast accommodations in private homes for either a membership or placement fee or at no cost to you at all.

Architecture and Period

The California concept of the b&b ranges architecturally from an 1872 brandy distillery to a ranch-style suburban home with swimming pool to a sprawling 1906 Edwardian house with breathtaking urban views. In other words, you'll find a bed & breakfast representative of almost every type of California's architecture whether it be turn-of-the-century, Gothic, Tudor, early frontier, contemporary, or brand new built to "look" old. You'll also discover bed & breakfasts with unusual historic uses, such as a former fishery, a 1920s yacht club, a hospital, a tree house nestled in the woods, and a former bordello.

Furnishings and Accessories

Just as the architecture of California bed & breakfasts varies, the furnishings within also provide variety and, sometimes, surprises. Many b&b travelers assume bed & breakfast is equivalent to "antique." True, many of the bed & breakfasts concentrate on recreating the past in California, often consistent with the establishment's turn-of-the-century or late 1800s vintage. But some bed & breakfast owners choose an eclectic decorating style, often blending harmoniously the old and new to create a very individual feel. Some establishments feature guest rooms that not only carry out different themes, but offer quite different decors. One Gold Country inn accomplishes this by offering some rooms in antiques, some with very contemporary furnishings, and others that are just "unique," with hanging beds that swing you to sleep. Representing a handful of totally contemporary establishments is one exceptional Victorian b&b in San Francisco whose surprisingly contemporary interior could be in an issue of *Architectural Digest*—an exciting contrast to say the least!

Family heirlooms, pottery or paintings, and the innkeeper's hobbies, such as a rare doll collection, add a personal touch to many establishments. Though the decor is endlessly varied, you'll find a common element in all the bed & breakfasts statewide: a desire to provide a hospitable and comfortable environment, whether it be accomplished with fresh flowers, candy, a decanter of wine or sherry, fresh fruit, bright and cheerful wallcoverings, or soft and inviting colors and patterns.

3

Bed & Breakfast Settings

The "country inn" is synonymous with the bed & breakfast concept, but many of California's b&bs have sprung up in the city and downtown areas. These "urban inns" are a mixture of hotels and former factories turned bed & breakfast, large homes or mansions, rowhouses, and even private homes offering a room or two. Convenience is the keyword in this urban setting for the tourist and the businessperson alike. Fine restaurants, civic centers, shopping, and cultural events are often just a walk away. Many of the city establishments that were once hotels also offer a wider range of services such as telephones, television, and business-meeting facilities.

Nestled among lilacs and ancient oaks, perched atop a mountain with patchwork fields stretched out for miles, or ensconced in a peaceful suburban neighborhood, the bed & breakfast in the country offers diverse, and often rural, settings. Many western ranches in the state have adopted bed & breakfast traits while also offering the ranch-style amenities of animals, casual dress, and hearty meals. California's rapidly growing wine industry goes hand in hand with its expanding b&b business, as shown not only in the number of bed & breakfasts surrounding wineries, but also by the many b&bs on the vineyard grounds. What could be more unique to California bed & breakfast travel than the opportunity to sleep and breakfast among verdant vines and oak barrels, sampling the latest harvest in your room before retiring?

Residential area b&bs range from tree-lined Victorian neighborhoods to a California 1950s tract to a custom wood-and-glass structure reaching out to the Pacific Ocean. You'll find large mansions and estates and modest private homes located in all sorts of residential areas, some more rural than others, but all with something special to offer.

FINDING THE RIGHT
BED & BREAKFAST

Scouting the Whereabouts of Bed & Breakfasts

The Directory in this book is the most complete guide currently available to bed & breakfast establishments in California. Of course, new b&bs are opening constantly as this idea gains greater and greater popularity from seashore to desert, from mountains to cities. For that reason, if you care to stay completely abreast of new finds, you'll want to keep a watchful eye on other sources as well.

Travel Publications

To the delight of bed & breakfast travelers, travel articles in newspapers and magazines are focusing more and more on bed & breakfast developments these days. Many new establishments gain their audience this way, so openings are often announced in travel editors' columns or the "Letters to the Travel Editor" section on Sunday. By far the most useful and current is Jerry Hulse's *Los Angeles Times* travel section each Sunday. Both Mr. Hulse's column and letters section are, more often than not, sprinkled with the latest in b&b openings and reader reviews.

A few newsletters devoted to bed & breakfast happenings in California have emerged recently. One publication that reports new b&b openings and closures and reviews selected establishments is *California Inns* by Toby Smith. An annual subscription (ten issues) costs twenty-five dollars and can be obtained by writing to Ms. Smith at P.O. Box 3383, Santa Rosa, CA 95402.

Tourist Bureaus

If you're traveling to a specific area and want an update on possible new bed & breakfasts, a call, letter, or visit to the local chamber of commerce or tourist center is usually a good start. These offices keep up with new businesses in general, especially those that cater to the tourist. Often they will distribute a brochure, if available, on the inn.

A knowledgeable travel agent will scout out a b&b at a client's request or maybe even make a suggestion of one for a special trip. Although many travel agents are not deterred by the fact that most California b&bs do not currently give a commission for the booking, some may be influenced by this fact. If your trip is being planned by a travel agent, you may want to do the suggesting. You will find, however, that many of the larger b&bs will offer travel-agent commissions.

Referrals

Following the Directory in this book is a listing of referral agencies based in California and primarily involved in b&b accommodations within the state. These referral agencies work in a variety of ways: Some choose to charge the inn or homeowner for each room they book; others require a membership fee, usually annual, which gives the member a descriptive listing of their offerings from which to choose; and still others sell the listings only, and you handle the booking arrangements. Some of these referral agencies deal with selected inns only, but a majority offer listings in private homes. Indeed, more home b&bs choose this alternative rather than soliciting guests on their own. The private homes listed in this Directory are those that do not rely solely upon a referral agency for their trade.

The bed & breakfast associations also listed following the Directory in this book are organizations formed by the innkeepers within that region. The associations have many and varied functions, such as forming standard guidelines for membership inns, advertising jointly, offering referrals, and so on, but all of the groups mentioned in this guide publish or give out the names of their association members. Most of these associations will send you a brochure or pamphlet with the names and descriptions of their member inns and require only that you first send a self-addressed stamped envelope.

Of course, let's not overlook the very valuable "personal referral" when searching for new b&bs. Bed & breakfasts survive mainly on word of mouth, and a new establishment's opening spreads among innkeepers and avid b&b-goers like fresh butter on a steaming hot croissant. So when staying at a bed & breakfast, talk to your fellow guests and pump your innkeeper for new information. It's by far the most delightful way to enlarge your Directory.

If becoming a bed & breakfast sleuth is not your cup of tea, then the solution to keeping current is simple—just watch your bookstore carefully for the next updated edition of *Bed & Breakfast in California!* Even you super-sleuths may find a few more.

What You Should Ask About a Bed & Breakfast

What could be less personal than dialing some anonymous person two thousand miles away on an even more anonymous "800" number and reserving a room in a chain motel by answering a quick, memorized list of questions? We have all performed this rather mindless act (perhaps hundreds of times), and it is simple to guess we are apt to receive the same impersonal greeting upon our arrival. We know what the room will look like except for the rather unexciting surprise of what the color scheme will be this time. If guessing the color of the bedspread and drapes is the most intrigue you derive from travel, then you're in for *thrills* traveling b&b style in California! Right from the moment you place your first call or receive a handwritten response to your inquiry, you'll discover researching b&bs is not only easy to do, but fun at the same time—as long as you know what sorts of things to ask. For, before traveling to California bed & breakfasts, you get to ask the questions and mold your stay into the adventure and experience you've been longing for.

Description of the B&B

By studying the Directory in this book, you may have a good idea which establishments in any given area you would like to know more about. If time allows, you may want to write a note briefly stating your specific questions; or if you are in a hurry, you will want to call the establishment directly and speak with the innkeeper or clerk. In either case, you will most likely be delighted with the very personal and warm response you receive. A common trait among innkeepers is their basic fondness for people, and this results in a gracious and helpful attitude. They are eager to answer your smallest question. If you telephone your innkeeper at a busy moment (the phone always rings when he or she is just about to serve ten guests with perfect three-minute eggs), ask him or her to call you back. Generally the busiest times are during breakfast and early evening, but since some innkeepers close at midday to take care of cleaning, shopping, washing, and the like, it is difficult to guess the best time to call—just keep trying.

Whether writing or phoning, be sure to request a brochure, rate card, post card, or whatever descriptive pieces are available. A brochure is the b&b's best tool for informing you and saving both of you time. One of the most common questions an innkeeper hears is "Can you tell me about your Inn?" Because the very nature of bed & breakfast is its uniqueness and individuality throughout, from its handsewn quilts to its stuffed teddy bear collection, the question can be overwhelming. In comes the brochure, the most convenient and descriptive way of telling you about all of the little extras, as well as the cost, rules, and policies.

Accommodations

Although the trend in California b&bs is oversized beds (king or queen) due to guests' demands in the last few years, you may want to double-check just in case a larger bed is important to you or if you prefer twin beds. Some inns have compromised by putting a larger bed and twin in the same room, which also satisfies requests for three to a room. But this situation is not common, and rollaways are not always available, so be sure to check. Some inns will offer a special rate for three traveling together in exchange for allowing three to a room, especially during nonpeak times. No matter what the size, comfort is usually a foremost consideration, and the beds are often outfitted with delicate sheets and plump comforters for an unforgettable night's rest.

Shared Baths: Those about to venture into b&b travel for the first time are usually the most hesitant about the next topic: the "shared bath." It actually prevents some from experiencing many places they would have otherwise cherished. "Shared bath" is not as easily defined as "private bath" because there are several degrees of "sharing" to be found. For instance, many shared-bath accommodations have within the guest room itself a "vanity area," generally consisting of a sink, mirror, plug-in, and appropriate towels and soap. Vanity areas cut down considerably on the use of the baths by allowing you to complete the more time-consuming tasks of make-up application, shaving, toothbrushing, hairstyling, and so on in your own room. If sharing the bath worries you, be sure to ask about the ratio of rooms to a bath. Often it is as low as two rooms to one bath or perhaps four rooms to a bath, but even the latter is rarely a problem. Remember, too, that bed & breakfast travelers are, for the most part, a very considerate lot who know to leave the bath promptly and as neat as when they entered. If you're still skittish most establishments do offer some private, if not all private, bath accommodations. But if you do insist on a private bath, be sure to peek at the shared baths before you leave. You may be pleasantly surprised to find them more elegant and spacious or decorated more authentically in claw-foot tubs, pedestal sinks, and pullchain toilets. A few California inns offer twin claw foots for bathing side by side!

Handicapped: Many cities and counties in California have adopted strict building and operating requirements for the handicapped guest at bed & breakfast inns, but the rules are far from uniform and rarely apply to private residences. If climbing stairs is the main concern, be sure to specify downstairs accommodations if available.

Rules and Policies

You'll discover many similarities in the rules and general policies of bed & breakfast establishments throughout the state. But you're also sure to find some exceptions and "bending of the rules." Bed & breakfasts can do that since they're dealing on such a personal level. The more professional the establishment, however, the more rigid they will tend to be regarding key policies, especially those regarding smoking, children, and pets, which affect other guests.

Children: There is nothing more disappointing when escaping from the children for a romantic getaway at an adult inn than to discover you're sharing breakfast with someone else's darlings. The soft-hearted innkeeper weakened and made an exception to the "no children" rule. This does happen occasionally, but usually "no children" means no children. A great number of California bed & breakfasts do not allow children under the age of sixteen or thirteen, but a few b&bs in every area welcome small children. If you are traveling with an infant or toddler, be sure to inquire even if the information you're reading states "children allowed." Many of the "children allowed" establishments draw the line at babies. If you're discovering bed & breakfast travel with the whole family, take heart; there are many wonderful accommodations to explore, and the result will be an exciting experience for all of you. It is important to understand that the bed & breakfast that does not allow small children often chooses this policy for the very reasons you enjoy this form of travel—the quiet, relaxing atmosphere free of disturbances and the delicate antiques, bric-a-brac, and fabrics. (Note: *The state is currently looking into the contention that not allowing children is discriminatory. To avoid this controversy, many establishments now say that children over a certain age are welcome rather than refusing children under a certain age. Please check carefully with your b&b on this issue.*)

Smoking: Smoking is a controversial subject everywhere these days. Many b&bs do not allow smoking inside at all, while others permit smoking in specific rooms only. This policy should be spelled out in the establishment's literature, but if not, be sure to ask. If you are a smoker, please abide by the rules of the house

9

to avoid embarrassment to yourself or your obliging innkeeper. Try to keep in mind that a no-smoking policy is often due to a variety of factors that include the protection and longevity of delicate fabrics and expensive antiques as well as the close proximity of areas and the general risks involved.

Pets: There are few exceptions to the "no pet" rule at bed & breakfasts in California. If you plan to travel with a pet, be sure to ask in advance. Unless otherwise stated in the descriptive material on each listing, pets are not allowed.

Days and Hours of Operation, Minimum Stays

Some bed & breakfasts operate nearly as motels/hotels: open seven days a week, management on duty twenty-four hours and so forth, but this is far from the norm. Indeed, some are open only when business is there, some on weekends only, and some only during certain seasons. Therefore it is important to determine if a particular establishment is open for business when you care to visit, as well as if a minimum stay is required. It is not unusual for a b&b to require a minimum stay of two nights during peak times: weekends, holidays, and special local events. Also, it is critical to indicate your approximate time of arrival so that proper arrangements are made for your check-in, especially if you are arriving later or earlier than the establishment's normal check-in timetable.

Rates

If you're traveling bed & breakfast style in California on the premise that you'll save a lot of money—sorry! You will discover that California inns are actually very similar in cost to the nicer motels in the same area, but don't overlook all of the extras you receive traveling b&b style. You probably will decide it is a bargain of sorts. Also, the rates in private homes are generally less expensive than the local motels, so genuine bargains do exist.

Some bed & breakfasts charge a flat fee per room, while others will give a separate rate for single occupancy, this averaging about five dollars less than the double fee. Since commercial business is not the mainstay of most bed & breakfast establishments, many do not offer commercial rates. If you are traveling on business, do make the request. More and more establishments are beginning to realize the value of the business patron and are offering a special rate, especially in urban areas and on weekdays.

It is not unusual for a bed & breakfast to offer special room rates at different times of the year: lower mid-week rates, winter or off-season reductions, weekly discounts, or holiday increases.

Often this information is not stated on the rate card, so be sure to inquire.

The tax imposed on lodging in California is referred to as "bed tax," and this tax amount varies from area to area, ranging anywhere from 3 percent to 10 percent of the room rate. Rates quoted for bed & breakfast accommodations are generally "without tax," so be sure to ask for the total amount when making advance payment for your lodging.

Deposits: In order to secure a reservation, many establishments require that the first night's stay be paid in advance; others require that the entire stay be paid before arrival. When credit cards are accepted, the credit card number can usually be taken for confirmation. It is important to ask what form of payment is acceptable at your bed & breakfast since many establishments deal only in cash and checks.

Cancellations: Since a majority of bed & breakfasts in California operate on a relatively small scale in comparison to hotels and motels, they must also impose much stricter cancellation policies. Most of the b&bs offer a total refund if a cancellation is made within a certain amount of time prior to your stay, ranging from forty-eight hours to five days. The cancellation policy should be stated clearly in the establishment's literature; if it isn't, be sure to ask. If circumstances require that you cancel your reservation at the last minute, do notify your b&b immediately. If your room can be booked, then you will not be charged. If the room remains vacant, you may be charged, although most innkeepers will be lenient for extenuating circumstances or may move your stay to another agreed date. A handful of b&bs will charge you a cancellation fee for time and trouble regardless of when the cancellation was made.

Other Considerations

Breakfast: Breakfast is of course a common element in all of the b&bs around, but it can take many delicious forms. The most popular version of the California breakfast might be called an "extended continental breakfast," consisting of juice, fruit, coffee or tea, and baked goods. A "full" breakfast might add eggs, pancakes, waffles, or crepes to the above; a simpler continental fare might delete the fresh fruit. The important factor here in choosing your bed & breakfast might not be "how much," but rather "how well" it is prepared and served. Often a b&b will vary its menu, which makes for scrumptious variety each time you visit.

If *where* breakfast is served is important to you, be sure to ask. Many establishments with a dining room serve all guests

11

there during a certain period of time, such as from 8:00 A.M. to 10:00 A.M. Some offer both the dining room (or parlor) as well as in-room service, while others offer only the latter. Some b&bs literally offer "breakfast in bed," but most in-room breakfasts are served on a table provided in the room at a specific time. Breakfast in your room can be fun, but many avid b&b travelers delight in the communal dining situation that allows for interesting exchanges with fellow guests and innkeepers.

Refreshments: Although it's not a requirement for being defined as a bed & breakfast, many b&bs in California offer refreshments apart from breakfast; and they have found many creative ways of accomplishing this pleasant repast. You'll discover anything from wine and hors d'oeuvres in the evening to an in-room basket of goodies to cookies and tea at midday. (Note: *The ABC is currently setting guidelines for the service of alcoholic beverages on a complimentary basis in bed & breakfasts throughout the state. Some inns have been forced to suspend this offering and switch to nonalcoholic beverages, and others may follow suit in coming months.*)

Televisions, Telephones, and Transportation: Contrary to common belief, some California b&bs do have television in the rooms, but they are certainly the exception and usually fall into the Inn/Hotel category. More commonly, if television is available on the premises, it will be found in a lounge area.

Telephones also are found more commonly in the Inn/Hotel situation and are a rarity in b&bs, but they are sometimes available to guests by mobile phone units, phone jacks, pay phones, or guest phones located in a common area.

Since most b&bs are small operations, pickup service is often not available, but some do offer transportation from airports, train depots, or bus stations with prior notice. Those that do not are usually happy to assist in arranging alternative ways of getting you there via bus or taxi. Parking availability at your b&b is an important question, especially at those in San Francisco or other larger city areas where there may be an additional charge for parking.

Special Arrangements

Bed & breakfasts with all their inherent charm are catching on as attractive places to hold small functions such as weddings, receptions, business retreats, and reunions. Some establishments do not encourage group functions, while others are eager to arrange and assist in the various details.

Because California b&bs provide ideal settings for special times such as birthdays, honeymoons, and anniversaries, many establishments offer champagne or some other very special provision, often on a complimentary basis, with prior notice. If you are staying on such an occasion, be sure to mention it when making your reservation.

Gift certificates are becoming a very popular offering of California b&bs. There are some very attractive certificates available, and you may decide it's a perfect gift idea for a relative, friend, or work associate.

RESERVE, PACK AND ARRIVE
WITH CONFIDENCE—THEN ENJOY

Reserving, Confirming and Arriving

When traveling bed & breakfast style in California, a reservation is almost a must in that some establishments operate only on advance reservations, but all prefer and recommend that method. Don't allow this fact to dissuade you from a spur-of-the-moment trip, because cancellations do occur, and b&bs need a high occupancy rate to survive. Do make it a habit to reserve as early as possible to avoid disappointment, however, since it is not unusual for a b&b to be booked several weeks (even months) ahead, especially on weekends. Not only are you apt to obtain a reservation early, but you will also have a better pick of the guest accommodations: that cozy fireplace room or the bed that "the general" slept in.

The Reservation and Deposit

You may reserve your room by phone or mail, but in either case be specific. Less confusion is apt to arise if you choose to phone, which allows for clear, immediate deposit instructions from your b&b, back-up room selections, and a quick acknowledgment of a vacancy. Once an accommodation is decided upon, the next step is the deposit that will secure your reservation. Many establishments, especially those that do not accept credit cards, require either the first night's tariff or the amount for the entire stay in advance. On the average this amount is due within five to seven days from the date the reservation is made. If you forget, you may discover your room has been given away. On your deposit check be sure to indicate the dates of your stay as a cross-check and easy reference. If your b&b accepts credit cards, usually VISA or MasterCard, then often the number and date of expiration will hold your reservation. If you need to cancel and do not notify your innkeeper, do not be surprised to find the amount on your next charge-account statement. In defense of bed & breakfasts, every room is crucial to financial prosperity when working on such a small scale, and b&bs are one of the few lodging establishments that will loyally hold that room for you no matter what unless they hear otherwise.

Confirmation and Arrival

Upon receiving your check or after noting your charge number, the b&b should send you a confirmation note, usually handwritten, along with a brochure if you do not already have one. Included somewhere should be the "rules of the house," and you should read these carefully, especially points regarding their cancellation policy, children, smoking, and check-in times.

When you reserve your room, make it clear what time you plan to arrive. Bed & breakfasts often close as early as 8:00 P.M. and may also close around midday. Late arrivals can usually be handled efficiently with advance warning; early arrivals may at least be able to leave luggage and freshen up with prior arrangements.

Another item to keep in mind when placing your reservation is advance tour or dinner arrangements that your b&b host might be happy to handle for you. If there is a special event or very popular dining spot in town, ask if the b&b would handle reservations for you ahead of time.

Emergency Provisions

As pleasant as bed and breakfast travel is in California, problems and emergencies can arise. To avoid a panic situation, be sure to acquaint yourself with emergency provisions upon checking in: Is there a resident manager? Where can he or she be found after closing time? Is an emergency phone available and where? If no resident manager is on the premises, how can the owners be reached? Are phone numbers posted? Ask whom you should see if you lose your key in the night or the toilet backs up or your next-door guests decide to have an all-night party. The chances are good that you will have a marvelous, romantic stay without a hint of a problem, but it is good to be prepared.

A common problem centers on the security of the b&b, which often involves locking doors up tight at a certain time of the night. If you find yourself arriving late without notifying the bed & breakfast, then look for a late box with a key or a number to call or just knock loudly! Of course, you should always call when possible if you're arriving later than the indicated office hours. If you're a guest already and you lose your key, the same applies. As a note, keys are handled quite differently at various establishments. Some issue you a key to your room and the front door, others just to the front door if your guest room has an inside latch. Still others deal with no keys at all. I know of a few inns with a curfew, but luckily those are a rarity—staying at "grandmother's" can be taken to extremes.

Checking Out

Most bed & breakfast check-outs, like motels and hotels, are at noon or 11:00 A.M. If you haven't paid in full, do so and also remember to return the keys. Always bid farewell personally and sign the guestbook if you like. It's great fun to read the guestbook, too. Should you tip? Some b&bs ask that you do not tip, but others leave that up to the guest; it is rarely expected. Do what pleases you, but add a name if the tip is for a specific person (otherwise the housekeeper may assume it is just for her). Some b&b travelers prefer more creative tipping such as a bottle of wine or a bouquet of flowers for the host. As a bed & breakfast owner, my favorite gratuity was always a heartfelt note of thanks with a promise to return.

Packing for Your Stay at a Bed & Breakfast

Just two words of advice here: Pack lightly! A recent California University survey on state bed & breakfasts reveals the average stay to be two nights, so most likely you won't pack for a week unless you're in transit. In that case, prepare ahead with a small suitcase for your b&b stop and leave the rest in the car. It is not at all unusual to discover your beautiful, antique-filled room is missing a closet, and in its place are a few ornate brass hooks or perhaps a tiny turn-of-the-century armoire. Of course, some b&bs have lovely, large closets, but you might want to check if you're traveling with an entire wardrobe.

Once you've determined how much to tote, you'll need to give thought to what to bring along. When you're sharing the bath, a robe of some sort is a necessity. Some gracious inns do supply a robe if you forget yours, but you wouldn't want to depend on that. A small cosmetic or toiletry bag for sundry items will also make your "trip down the hall" much more efficient and comfortable. Although most guest rooms will have a mirror, and indeed many are equipped with full vanity/sink areas, it is wise to carry a traveling standup mirror. Then, if the bath is occupied or you are nervous about taking a few extra minutes on your coiffure, you can proceed in the privacy of your room.

Many of the b&b inns and inn/hotels in California are, if not historic, definitely older—circa 1900. The turn-of-the-century renovated structures provide a unique and elegant stay, but they do not always provide impressive heating, air conditioning, plumbing, and electrical situations. This is not to say you will be uncomfortable; most likely you won't even notice. But if you chill or overheat easily, then pack a sweater or a few lighter pieces of clothing. Also, the use of higher voltage electrical appliances, such as your hair dryer, can be affected. If not using your blower would be a disaster, then you had better ask ahead.

If you plan to travel with a supply of cold drinks or refreshments and your accommodations do not include a refrigerator, then ask about using the establishment's own refrigerator. Some places will offer happily, while others prefer not to extend this service due to several factors. Motels and hotels have trained the California traveler into the "ice-machine habit," but not one such machine exists in the state's b&b offerings. A few of the larger inn/ hotels may have an ice dispenser, but your "ice machine" will most likely be a carton of cubes brought out graciously by the innkeeper at your request.

Enjoying Your Stay to the Fullest

The grand, spiraling staircase may conjure up childhood fantasies of sliding down its smooth walnut banister, and the painted, carved carousel horse in the parlor has your mind wandering to playful, simpler times. Yet a California bed & breakfast can do more than bring nostalgic thoughts to mind, especially if you prepare to enjoy all it has to offer.

Enjoying a bed & breakfast can be an end in itself, but often you'll want to explore its setting as well. As your own "personal tourist bureau," the b&b is ideally suited to recommend and even chart out a day's or week's activities. Many establishments are equipped with area brochures, maps, and, most importantly, an innkeeper or host with very knowledgeable ideas of what's worthwhile.

The Breakfast
The breakfast is a most enjoyable other half of the b&b; and it's great fun to discover the unique ways different establishments accomplish this meal. As discussed earlier, locales and types of breakfasts can vary from in-bed trays to formal dining rooms, from juice and croissants to homemade country feasts. To make the most of your breakfast, check your options and try several if you're staying longer than a day. Be sure to mention any special dietary requirement upon arrival. The personal touch at a b&b

17

mirrors the desire to please whenever possible. Don't be surprised to find a copy of the morning paper alongside your coffee cup.

Refreshments and Other Offerings

Picture yourself arriving at your bed & breakfast destination exhausted from a long drive; the next thing you know, a chilled glass of wine or a hot cup of tea is there to soothe your traveler's woes. Or perhaps you are escorted to your room to freshen up and presented with a basketed "care package" of fresh fruit or cookies. Or you go downstairs in the late afternoon to gather with fellow guests for champagne, hors d'oeuvres, and warm conversation. Many establishments now offer late-night snacks or after-dinner desserts. In any circumstance, the refreshment offering practiced by most California b&bs is a most enjoyable and refreshing gesture.

Breakfast is not necessarily the only meal offered at California bed & breakfasts. With advance notice many establishments will pack a homemade picnic lunch for your day's outing or will prepare a special gourmet dinner. Of course, many of the larger inn/hotels have their own adjoining restaurants that are open to guests and the public on a regular basis.

The Extras

The extra services you'll find at California b&bs are almost too numerous to mention, as you are sure to notice when reading the descriptions in this edition. In terms of recreation and relaxation, you'll find bicycles for exploring (both on a complimentary basis and rentals), spas, saunas, hot tubs, and pools—all a part of the California scene. Turn-of-the-century gazebos, lawn croquet, ponds, creeks, and flower-filled gardens abound in both country and urban settings. Some newly opened inns offer such extras as trolley rides, souvenir photos in historic costumes, bay cruises, and touring in vintage autos.

Within your bed & breakfast you'll almost always find some sort of sitting room, parlor, or library with comfy nooks, lots of reading material, and, at times, a television, radio, or player piano. These relaxation spots often feature a fireplace to sip by or challenging games for one or more.

The newest diversions at California's b&bs involve "theme" weekends. Guests may participate in a weekend-long mystery murder and rendezvous for clues at midnight at the gazebo; enjoy a real western barbecue and shoot-out in Gold Country, or be escorted through chocolate havens around Los Angeles.

More Than a Bubblebath

The shared baths at most b&bs are surveyed and neatened or cleaned several times during the day, but courtesy dictates some general guidelines for their use. If a can of spray cleaner and a sponge are in view, then do take it upon yourself to do a quick wipe after using the tub. If bubblebath is available, please use it. Lounging in bubbles up to your earlobes is not only luxurious, it also keeps the ugly ring from forming when the last bubble has disappeared. Many of the new private baths feature Jacuzzi tubs for some modern luxury.

Guest Room Frills

Within the privacy of your room, you may discover a decanter of sherry, fruit, or candies to fill your cravings. Many b&b accommodations include refrigerators, wet bars, and even whole kitchens for you to stock with your favorites. With an emphasis on comfort, it is not unusual to find yourself relaxing in beds donned with plush comforters, down pillows, and fancy sheets. Ask for extra blankets or pillows if you like. If you enjoy reading in bed, then ask for a reading light; ask for an alarm clock for a special wake-up time. If your room has a fireplace, check to be sure it's working and find out how to use it. Some establishments prefer to start your fire for you or may have simple instructions available. You may return from the evening out to discover a sweet elf has lovingly turned down your bed and left an elfin treat of candies or sherry, freshened your towels, and maybe even shined your shoes!

The Bed & Breakfast in California
Traveler's Checklist

1. Choosing your bed & breakfast
☐ *Request a brochure, rate card*
☐ *Check policies regarding smoking, children, credit cards, cancellations*
☐ *Minimum-stay requirement*
☐ *Days and hours of operation, arrival time*

2. Reserving with confidence
☐ *Total deposit required? When?*
☐ *Form of payment accepted*
☐ *Confirmation received*
☐ *Late or early arrival*
☐ *Advance tour or dinner reservations*
☐ *Parking*
☐ *How to get there*
☐ *Public transportation, pickup service*

3. Packing for your stay
☐ *Robe*
☐ *Tote*
☐ *Electrical appliances*

4. Checking in and out
☐ *Breakfast options*
☐ *Emergency provisions*
☐ *Office hours*
☐ *Keys*
☐ *Guestbook*

5. Enjoying your stay
☐ *Personal tourist information*
☐ *Refreshment time*
☐ *Picnics, lunches, dinners*
☐ *Bicycles*
☐ *Spas, saunas, pools, hot tubs*
☐ *Patios, gardens, gazebos*
☐ *Parlor/library: books, games, fireplaces, pianos*
☐ *Shared bath: bubblebath, robes, cleaning supplies*
☐ *Room comforts: reading lights, alarm clocks, extra pillows/ blankets, refreshments, fireplace use*
☐ *Telephone*
☐ *Television*

PART TWO

BED & BREAKFAST IN CALIFORNIA DIRECTORY

HOW TO USE THE DIRECTORY

Geographic Areas: All of the b&b establishments listed in the Directory have been categorized geographically into one of the following six areas, each displayed with a map highlighting pertinent communities and described in a brief list of things to do and see:

- **Northern California:** Northernmost California, primarily the north coast and redwood country
- **California Wine Country:** Napa and Sonoma Counties
- **California Gold Country:** Sacramento and adjoining Gold Country including Tahoe, the Sierra Foothills, and the Central Valley
- **San Francisco Bay Area:** The City and surrounding Bay communities
- **Central California:** Santa Cruz–Monterey Bay south through San Luis Obispo County and the San Joaquin and Owens valleys
- **Southern California:** Santa Barbara County south through San Diego

Individual Listings: Each bed & breakfast listing in the directory is followed by basic information about that particular b&b.

Reading the key:
1. Inn—Operates primarily as a bed & breakfast inn
2. Inn/Hotel—Is an inn as well as hotel, usually offering other services such as an adjoining restaurant
3. Cottage—Usually a small cottage in back of a home or an inn
4. Home—A private home renting from one to four rooms (Most bed & breakfast homes can be found by checking with the referral agencies at the end of this Directory.)
   Number of Guest Rooms: This is the total number of units available and may include cottages as well as suites.
   Rates: Rates have been categorized in the following fashion based upon double occupancy, on-season rates before tax:
   1. Inexpensive: up to $55
   2. Moderate: $56–$90
   3. Expensive: $91–$130
   4. Deluxe: $131 and up
   Smoking:
   1. OK—Permitted in general
   2. Limited—Permitted in certain rooms only

3. No—Not allowed inside the establishment (most establishments have provisions for *outside* smoking)

Children: This refers to children under the age of 16 unless stated otherwise. When traveling with infants and toddlers, check with each establishment carefully for permission.

Credit Cards: When credit cards are accepted, the most common cards are MasterCard and VISA. Check with the establishment if traveling with any other charge card.

Pets: This item is *not* listed, because almost all b&bs within do not allow pets. If pets are allowed, an indication of this may be listed in the description.

Additions: The blank spaces at the end of each section are for your personal b&b additions or comments.

NORTHERN CALIFORNIA

Rugged coastlines, isolated stretches, "Cape Cod" villages, steep mountains, giant redwoods, old lumber and fishing towns, and farmland are the essence of California's scenic northern section. The inland areas here, housing towns such as Boonville and Garberville, are marked by warmer, drier weather, orchards, and the mighty redwood forests. The Skunk train, which departs near coastal Fort Bragg, travels the redwood area as a popular tourist attraction. The nineteenth-century coastal towns of Mendocino and Little River offer dramatic cliffs with ocean-view bluffs, meadows, rocky beaches, and architecture reminiscent of a New England fishing village. Colorful gardens, artist's galleries and craft shops, water recreation, and bountiful driftwood collections are all a part of Northern California, a year-round travel destination.

The Lady Anne

902 14th Street, Arcata, CA 95521
Phone: (707) 822-2797
Key: Inn; 5 units; Inexpensive-Mod.; No smoking; Children on approval; Credit cards

Known historically as the "Stone House" since it was built by Wesley Stone in 1888, this stately Victorian inn sits on a prestigious location on a hill overlooking the town and bay. The Queen Anne architecture of the house is enhanced by leaded glass, interior redwood trim, and a glass-enclosed veranda. Guests are treated to an old-fashioned parlor with a grand piano and assorted games and to a sitting room, the site of afternoon tea before a cozy fire. The five guest rooms of the inn are individually decorated in antiques and quilts; two rooms boast views of the bay. The "Countess Mary Velma" is a separate suite available to families with children and has a small kitchen, private bath, and even a crib and toys. The remaining guest rooms in the inn share a bath. Breakfast is offered in the elegant dining room or at the kitchen oak table nestled next to the old woodstove.

The Plough and the Stars Country Inn, Arcata

The Plough and the Stars Country Inn

1800 27th Street, Arcata, CA 95521
Phone: (707) 822-8236
Key: Inn; 5 units; Inexpensive-Mod.; Limited smoking; No children under 12; No credit cards

This mid-1800s farmhouse was once the center of a one-hundred-and-forty-acre ranch and housed a local entrepreneur's family of fourteen children. The lovingly restored country inn sits on two acres filled with fruit trees, pastures, lawns, and gardens and is bordered on three sides by a working bulb farm abloom with lilies and daffodils. The two upstairs guest rooms share a bath and an upstairs sitting room with views of the southern pasture. Three guest rooms downstairs offer full baths with showers and range in style from a summer sleeping porch to an elegant Victorian-designed room with a cozy woodstove. A generous continental breakfast is served family style in the country kitchen. A full breakfast, available on request at an additional charge, is complimentary on Sunday mornings. Three common rooms filled with books, games, antiques, and country touches such a teddy bears and locally made baskets are for lounging and socializing.

The Carter House

1033 Third Street, Eureka, CA 95501
Phone: (707) 445-1390
Key: Inn; 7 units; Moderate-Exp.; Limited smoking; No children under 10; Credit cards

This b&b calls itself "a modern tribute to the splendor of Victorian architecture." The three-story new structure, built from 1884 house plans, is just that. Victorian furnishings, marble and hardwood floors, Oriental carpets, and fresh flowers decorate throughout, and the third-floor b&b rooms offer views of Old Town and the marina. A full gourmet breakfast is included in the stay as well as evening wine and hors d'oeuvres and after-dinner cookies and cordials. The main floor of the building houses an art gallery.

Chalet de France

1817 Williams Street, Eureka, CA 95501
Phone: (707) 443-6512/444-3144
Key: Home; 2 units; Deluxe; No smoking; No children; No credit cards

Perched atop a 3,000-foot mountain, this chalet commands unparalled panoramic views of the Pacific Ocean and is an hour's drive through forest from Eureka. The remote setting surrounded by a thousand miles of ranch and timberland brings a touch of "France," complete with its yodeling mountaineer host and Belgian hostess who specializes in French cuisine, to its chalet architecture befitting a Swiss-French villa. The interior of the chalet boasts rich woods, tole-painted detailings, and intricate carvings. One suite offers a queen-size French rococo brass bed and the other, an antique iron double bed. The walls are filled with original artwork and etchings, and antique firearms, cut crystal, and china decorate throughout. The full breakfasts include eight different main courses featuring such delights as eggs Benedict and omelettes à la Provence along with champagne, fresh fruit, juice, and freshly baked muffins and breads. The morning meal is served either in the dining room or on the south deck

Chalet de France, Eureka

with thirty-mile views. Extras at this gracious b&b include massages by the innkeeper, a licensed masseuse, and escorted drives around the ranchlands in the inn's antique 1928 automobiles. The b&b accepts advance reservations only.

Eagle House

Second & C streets, Eureka, CA 95501
Phone: (707) 442-2334
Key: Inn; 10 units; Moderate-Exp.; Smoking OK; Children OK; Credit cards

This b&b occupies the third and fourth floors of a renovated 1888 hotel and offers spectacular views of the bay and the city. The interior of the High Victorian Stick structure is rich in turn-of-the-century antiques, and the ten guest rooms offer private baths, some impressive fireplaces, quaint wallcoverings, and views. Guests enjoy a relaxing Jacuzzi and a complimentary continental breakfast, as well as wine and hors d'oeuvres in the evening. The historic building also houses an antique shop, two restaurants, and a "Galleria" of specialty shops.

Heuer's Victorian Inn

1302 E. Street, Eureka, CA 95501
Phone: (707) 442-7334
Key: Inn; 3 units; Moderate; Smoking OK; No children; Credit cards

This Victorian inn, built in 1894, was completely restored in 1980. The Rose Room offers a private bath, while the Blue and Gold rooms share a bath. Wine and cheese is offered each evening in the second-floor Library, and the continental breakfast is served in the kitchen. Guests may enjoy all areas on the first two floors of the house as their own.

House of Francis

1006 Second Street, Eureka, CA 95501
Phone: (707) 443-3632
Key: Home; 2 units; Inexpensive; Limited smoking; Children OK; No credit cards

Built in the late 1800s and moved to its site two blocks from the Carson Mansion several years ago, the b&b is near the shops of Old Town. This home can accommodate up to four adults and one child in its comfortable suites. The stay includes a full breakfast of two kinds of fruit and a choice of whole wheat waffles, blueberry muffins, fruit muffins, French toast, French pancakes or popovers, and a soufflé omelette. Guests enjoy wonderful in-town views of the bay and marina.

Iris Inn Bed & Breakfast

1134 "H" Street, Eureka, CA 95501
Phone: (707) 445-0307
Key: Inn; 4 units; Inexpensive; Limited smoking; Children OK;
Credit cards

A few blocks from Old Town is this elegantly restored Queen
Anne-Victorian b&b built for Humboldt's first county clerk.
Guests may relax on the large Colonial Revival porch or in the
sunny yard with flowering fruit trees. Inside, guests enjoy the
pleasant blending of contemporary art and Victorian antiques
throughout, a music room used as an art gallery, and library and
parlor both with fireplaces. The restored home also boasts a profusion of stained-glass windows and an elegant dining room. The
four guest rooms include one accommodation with private bath
and boast expertly arranged flowers. The full gourmet breakfast
with main courses such as crêpes, soufflés, quiche or omelettes,
berries and cream, juice, and baked pastries is served in the dining
room with fine china, crystal, and silver or in the privacy of the
guest room. An elegant afternoon tea and evening nightcap of
cordials and hand-dipped chocolate truffles is presented in the
parlor. Extras at Iris include the morning newspaper and bed turn-
down service; picnic baskets are available. The inn loves children
and accepts collect calls.

Old Town Bed & Breakfast Inn

1521 Third Street, Eureka, CA 95501
Phone: (707) 445-3951
Key: Inn; 5 units; Inexpensive-Mod.; No smoking; Children OK on
arrangement; Credit cards

Built in 1871, this inn was the original home of the Carson
family and is the last remaining structure of the Bay Mill. The
Greek Revival Victorian was moved to its present location near
the Carson Mansion in 1915. The restored inn offers five guest
rooms with private and shared baths; "Sumner's Room" boasts an
antique brass double bed, a view of the bay, and private bath. The
inn's decor combines period pieces with homey touches, and
every bed has its own teddy bear. The antique claw-foot tubs are

Old Town Bed & Breakfast Inn, Eureka

outfitted with bubble bath and "rubber duckies." The inn serves a country gourmet breakfast, with such specialties as "Timber Beast Breakfast Pie" and "Eggs Derelict," served in the woodstove-heated kitchen. Guests relax in the "Raspberry Parlor" by the fireplace for wine and cheese each evening.

The Stevens House

917 Third Street, Eureka, CA 95501
Phone: (707) 445-9080
Key: Inn; 4 units; Inexpensive-Mod.; Limited smoking; No children under 11; Credit cards

This small Victorian inn was built in 1890 and has recently been restored by the owners of the Carter House. Located in Old Town, the b&b offers four guest rooms decorated in antiques and with shared or private bath. Breakfast includes freshly squeezed orange juice, fresh fruit with cream, homemade bran muffins, and apple-almond tarts.

McCloud Guest House

P.O. Box 1510, 606 W. Colombero Drive, McCloud, CA 96057
Phone: (916) 964-3160
Key: Inn; 5 units; Moderate; Limited smoking; No children;
Credit cards

Giant oaks, pines, rose gardens, and lawns surround this 1907 country inn and restaurant on the lower slopes of Mount Shasta. The entire guest house has been restored to its turn-of-the-century elegance with wallpapers, original chandeliers, claw-foot tubs, and pedestal sinks. Upstairs, the five spacious guest rooms are furnished with antiques, reproductions of brass and white-iron queen-size beds, and original beveled mirrors. Each accommodation boasts its own bath and a sitting area, which opens into the guest parlor with fireplace and antique pool table. The continental breakfast of assorted fruit, pastries, juice, and coffee or tea is served in the upstairs parlor; sherry may be sipped in the parlor each evening. Four mountain bikes are available for afternoon rides; the inn is only six miles from Mt. Shasta Ski Park and near several golf courses and trout-fishing spots. The first floor of the guest house is a well-known dinner house open to the public Wednesday through Sunday; reservations are suggested.

Palisades Paradise

1200 Palisades Avenue, Redding, CA 96003
Phone: (916) 223-5305
Key: Home; 2 units; Inexpensive; Limited smoking; No children under 8; Credit cards

Just thirty feet from the banks of the Sacramento River in a quiet residential area is this contemporary home b&b with sixty-foot patio, redwood deck with spa overlooking the city and river, and well-groomed lawns. The two guest accommodations, professionally decorated with traditional furnishings, share one bath. The spacious "Sunset Suite" offers a sitting area and sliding glass doors to the back lawn and deck. Drinks and snacks are offered upon arrival, and the breakfast is served in the dining area with fresh flowers. The complete morning meal includes fresh fruit or juice, an egg dish with homemade Swedish coffeecake, or German pancakes with fruit. The b&b is a perfect retreat for outdoor enthusiasts; guests may choose to sit by a fire in the living room or relax on the old-fashioned porch swing under the oak tree.

The Ferndale Inn

619 Main Street, Ferndale, CA 95536
Phone: (707) 786-4307
Key: Inn; 4 units; Inexpensive-Mod.; Smoking OK; Children OK; Credit cards

Built in 1859 as the third house in Ferndale, the structure was nicknamed the "Carpenter Gothic" because of its unique style. The Victorian grounds include a 100-year-old spreading chestnut tree; a large, colorful flower garden; and a redwood deck overlooking Francis Creek. Accommodations at the inn feature a suite with queen bed, carved oak headboard, sundeck, and full bath, as well as both shared- and private-bath guest rooms. Guests may relax in the parlor with nineteenth-century antiques or in the music room with an 1880 pump organ and varied antique instruments. The dining room, in turn-of-the-century decor, is the site for breakfast, which features freshly squeezed orange juice, fruit salad, hard-boiled eggs, fresh onion-cheese bread, coffeecake, honey bran muffins, and more. Tea and cookies or wine and cheese are served each afternoon at the inn, and bedstand treats include hand-dipped truffles.

The Gingerbread Mansion

400 Berding Street, Ferndale, CA 95536
Phone: (707) 786-4000
Key: Inn; 8 units; Moderate; No smoking; No children under 10; Credit cards

This storybook Queen Anne–Eastlake-style Victorian mansion with turrets, gables, and "gingerbread" galore is surrounded by colorful English gardens. Guests enjoy the turn-of-the-century elegance of four parlors with two fireplaces and eight large and romantic guest rooms. Five of the guest accommodations boast

The Gingerbread Mansion, Ferndale

private baths, and two feature claw-foot tubs in the room. The "Gingerbread Suite" offers *two* tubs for "his and her" bubble baths! Before-breakfast trays of coffee and tea may be enjoyed in the room. A generous continental breakfast is served in the formal dining room overlooking the garden. Guests at this inn are pampered with afternoon tea and cakes, bicycles for exploring, chocolates, bath robes and bubble bath, and even boots and umbrellas when it rains!

The Shaw House Inn

703 Main Street, Ferndale, CA 95536
Phone: (707) 786-9958
Key: Inn; 5 units; Moderate; No smoking; No children; No credit cards

This gabled, Gothic-style house was built by the town's founder in 1854. The exterior is enhanced by two old-fashioned porches, bays, and numerous balconies. Rooms inside are decorated in wallcoverings, antiques, art and memorabilia. The "honeymoon" room has a private bath and special honeymoon bed. Tea is served fireside in the library, and breakfast is presented on fine china in the formal dining room.

Scotia Inn

P.O. Box 248, Scotia, CA 95565
Phone: (707) 764-5683
Key: Inn; 10 units; Moderate-Exp.; Limited smoking; Children OK; Credit cards

Surrounded by forested hills and nestled along the Eel River, this historic inn has been in operation since 1888. Beautifully renovated in 1985, the b&b boasts a polished redwood lobby with comfortable seating and ten guest rooms, each with private bath. The spacious guest accommodations include king- and queen-size beds, antiques, European silk wallcoverings, and original clawfoot tubs. The "Bridal Suite" features an adjoining Jacuzzi room. The homemade continental breakfast is served in the lobby from 7:30 A.M. to 10:00 A.M. and complete dining, cocktail, and banquet facilities are available.

Dinsmore Lodge and Ranch

Dinsmore, CA 95526
Phone: (707) 574-6466
Key: Inn/Cottages; 30 units; Inexpensive-Mod.; Smoking OK; Children OK; Credit cards

This old-fashioned resort was built at the turn of the century as a stagecoach stop. Nestled amid tall timbered mountains and wildflowers, the inn offers antiques and memorabilia throughout its main-lodge guest rooms, cabins, and guest houses. The grounds feature a river "swimming hole," hiking, fishing, badminton, croquet, and horseshoes. Guests enjoy a private dining room for all their meals.

The Faulkner House

1029 Jefferson Street, Red Bluff, CA 96080
Phone: (916) 529-0520
Key: Inn; 4 units; Inexpensive-Mod.; Limited smoking; No children; No credit cards

This beautiful Queen Anne–Victorian home on a vintage tree-lined street still retains its original molding, leaded-glass windows, and outside porches. Guests are invited to enjoy the round sitting room/parlor, the living room, and the dining room, all tastefully decorated in antiques. The guest rooms also are furnished in period pieces and feature old-fashioned high ceilings. The "Arbor Room" boasts a European-carved bedroom set and private bath; the "Wicker Room" is sunny and light; the "Tower Room" is cozy; and the "Rose Room" features a brocade fainting couch. The three accommodations share baths. A light snack of wine, fruit, and cheese is served to guests upon arrival. The morning meal, offered from 8:00 A.M. to 9:00 A.M. in the dining room, includes fresh fruit, orange juice, and breads or croissants.

Cobweb Palace Inn

P.O. Box 132, 38921 N. Highway One, Westport, CA 95488
Phone: (707) 964-5588
Key: Inn; 6 units; Inexpensive-Mod.; Smoking OK; No children under 14; Credit cards

This western Victorian inn, reminiscent of the 1890s, also has an old-time dining room for full-course dinners at an additional charge and a beer-and-wine bar. Guest rooms, located in the inn and in an annex building, offer views of the sea and mountains in this remote setting; some have balconies. The continental breakfast included in the stay consists of fresh fruit, homemade muffins, preserves, and juice. The inn is located just 200 yards from the ocean.

Howard Creek Ranch, Westport

Howard Creek Ranch

P.O. Box 121, 40501 N. Highway One, Westport, CA 95488
Phone: (707) 964-6725
Key: Inn/Cottages; 7 units; Inexpensive-Mod.; Limited smoking;
Children on arrangement; No credit cards

Rolling mountains, wide sandy beaches, and tranquility surround this ranch, which was first settled in the 1870s. The New
England-style inn is full of antiques and memorabilia. Rooms feature views of the ocean or mountains and private or shared baths.
Recreation includes a hot tub, sauna, and pool nestled in the
ranch hillside with superior views. A full ranch breakfast featuring eggs, sausage, hot cakes, and bacon is served in the dining
room on antique table settings.

Blue Rose Inn

520 N. Main Street, Fort Bragg, CA 95437
Phone: (707) 964-3477
Key: Inn; 5 units; Moderate; No smoking; No children; Credit
cards

This intimate and informal inn offers spacious guest rooms with private baths. A homey atmosphere is achieved with abundant stained glass and brass, warm carpets, redwood moldings, and antique accents. Guests enjoy privacy and quiet in the b&b's colorful "tea gardens." A full breakfast is included in the stay.

Cleone Lodge

24600 N. Highway One, Fort Bragg, CA 95437
Phone: (707) 964-2788
Key: Inn/Cottage; 11 units; Inexpensive-Mod.; Smoking OK; Children OK; Credit cards

Located in a rustic lumbering area, this ranch-style country inn is situated on five and one-half wooded acres conducive to strolling and relaxation. Lodge guest rooms, with private baths, have cabinlike interiors; some offer fireplaces, kitchens, sitting areas, TV, antiques, and decks. A separate country cottage and beach house are also available. This lodge "becomes" a b&b establishment with an optional plan of services that can include, along with the continental breakfast, a hot tub and beverage and snack service.

Country Inn

632 North Main Street, Fort Bragg, CA 95437
Phone: (707) 964-3737
Key: Inn; 8 units; Moderate; No smoking; No children under 15; Credit cards

The early 1890s-built home, within walking distance to town and the Skunk Railroad, has been beautifully renovated. All guest rooms boast king- or queen-size beds, private baths (one with an antique claw-foot tub), wallpapers, and colorful touches. The redwood sun deck and skylighted sitting room with potbelly stove and art pieces are there for the guests' relaxation. A glass of complimentary wine is served each evening, and morning brings homebaked fruit and nut breads; hot honey, corn, or bran muffins; and fresh fruit.

Glass Beach Bed & Breakfast Inn

726 North Main Street, Fort Bragg, CA 95437
Phone: (707) 964-6774
Key: Inn; 9 units; Moderate; Smoking OK; No children; Credit cards

This 1920s renovated home offers uniquely decorated guest accommodations both upstairs and down. Rooms range from an Asian-wicker motif to a Victorian attic room; all have private baths with shower/tub combinations. The sitting room with reading material and games is the locale of evening wine and snacks, as well as the generous breakfast, which also may be taken to the room. Guests enjoy a private hot tub.

The Grey Whale Inn, Fort Bragg

The Grey Whale Inn

615 North Main Street, Fort Bragg, CA 95437
Phone: (707) 964-0640/(800) 382-7244
Key: Inn; 14 units; Moderate-Exp.; Smoking OK; No children under 12; Credit cards

Built in 1915 in the classic style of old-growth redwood, this stately, historic building served as the Redwood Coast Hospital until 1971 but leaves no hint of its former identity. The carefully renovated inn boasts beveled glass, interesting local art throughout, and rich carpeting. The spacious and airy guest rooms offer views of the town and hills or the ocean, as well as private baths; a favorite is the "Fireside Rendezvous Room." A new honeymoon suite boasts a special bath with soaking tub. Guests gather in the ground-floor recreation room for games or in the parlor for menus and touring information. The delightful breakfast buffet includes juices, seasonal fruit, homemade coffee cakes, cereal, and a special entree that may range from egg-and-sausage casserole to bacon-and-egg breakfast pie.

Noyo River Lodge

500 Casa del Noyo Drive, Fort Bragg, CA 95437
Phone: (707) 964-8045
Key: Inn/Cottage; 6 units; Moderate; No smoking; Children OK; Credit cards

This inn was originally built in 1868 as a residence and reveals the fine woodwork and craftsmanship of the period throughout. Situated on two and one-half acres of cypress trees and flower gardens, the b&b overlooks the Noyo River and village. Guest accommodations include spacious, carpeted guest rooms with antique private baths, antique furnishings and views, and an attached vine-covered cabin with a king-size bed, skylights, and fireplace. The continental breakfast is served in the main lodge building, which has two fireplaces in its lounge and restaurant.

Pudding Creek Inn

700 North Main Street, Fort Bragg, CA 95437
Phone: (707) 964-9529
Key: Inn; 10 units; Inexpensive-Mod.; Limited smoking; No children under 10; Credit cards

Two 1884 Victorian homes connected by an enclosed garden court make up this b&b. Each guest room is uniquely decorated in a country-style motif; all offer private baths, some with original turn-of-the-century fixtures, and two feature working fireplaces. Guests breakfast on homemade coffee breads, fruit, and juice among the begonias and ferns in the courtyard. This setting is also the site of complimentary evening wine. A small country store with gifts and antiques is located in one of the houses.

The Doll House Bed & Breakfast

118 School Street, Willits, CA 95490
Phone: (707) 459-4055
Key: Inn; 3 units; Moderate; Limited smoking; No children under 12; No credit cards

This restored Queen Anne cottage is just one block from Main Street and walking distance to shops and the Skunk Train Depot. The gingerbread-laden house, surrounded by colorful flowering shrubs and gardens, offers guest rooms with cheery wallcoverings and handmade quilts. The downstairs room features a private bath, and the two upstairs bedrooms, oversized, offer quaint dormer windows. Guests enjoy a dining room with nearby antique piano, a living room with bay window and period furniture, and the "Doll Room" filled with more than 500 dolls that overflow into other rooms of the house. The full, country-style breakfast served on fine china includes such delicacies as fresh orange juice, bacon and sausage, scrambled ranch eggs, bran muffins, homemade jam, and coffee or tea; early morning beverage and newspaper are delivered to each guest room.

Agate Cove Inn, Mendocino

Agate Cove Inn

P.O. Box 1150, 11201 Lansing Street, Mendocino, CA 95460
Phone: (707) 937-0551/(800) 527-3111 (CA)
Key: Inn/Cottages; 10 units; Inexpensive-Exp.; Limited smoking;
No children under 13; No credit cards

When guests check into this tiny "village" of Cape Cod–style cottages surrounding an 1860s-built farmhouse, they receive a complimentary bottle of wine from the innkeeper to enjoy on their own cottage deck. The main house, built by the first brewer of Mendocino Beer in the country, is the innkeeper's residence as well as the locale of the sumptuous breakfast of omelettes, blueberry or buttermilk pancakes with sausage or ham, or Agate Cove's own French toast or eggs Benedict. Guests enjoy this repast while viewing the splendor the crashing waves below. Each individual cottage, painted an ocean blue with white trim, features quaint wallcoverings above the wainscoting, a four-poster bed, cozy fireplace, color TV, and private bath (some with double tubs or double showers). Fresh flowers and ocean views past red passion vines and marigolds make these cottages extra special.

Ames Lodge, Mendocino

Ames Lodge

P.O. Box 207, 42287 Little Lake Road, Mendocino, CA 95460
Phone: (707) 937-0811
Key: Inn; 7 units; Inexpensive-Mod.; Limited smoking; Children
OK; No credit cards

This rustic redwood lodge surrounded by firs, redwoods, wild rhododendrons, mushrooms, birds, and deer has been a b&b lodge for more than twenty years. It was originally built by composer William Ames as a retreat for his fellow poets and musicians. Just three miles east of the village of Mendocino, the inn is casual and comfortable and offers a common room with a fireplace, library, and stereo for guests' use. The help-yourself breakfast of home-made, whole-grain breads or muffins and fresh fruit salad is offered here as well between 9:00 A.M. and 10:00 A.M. each day. The seven guest rooms, two with private baths, contain queen-size beds and some beamed ceilings. Families are welcome at this reasonable, rural retreat.

B.G. Ranch and Inn, Mendocino

B. G. Ranch and Inn

9601 Highway One, Mendocino, CA 95460
Phone: (707) 937-5322
Key: Inn; 4 units; Inexpensive-Mod.; Limited smoking; Children
OK; No credit cards

This coastal ranch house, built in the late 1800s, is surrounded by fourteen acres of redwood forest, gardens, and meadows and overlooks the inn's own stream-fed pond and wildlife-filled woods. The upstairs of the house consists of two bedrooms for guests that share a bath and offer such detailing as the original polished redwood floors, picture-window views, and skylights. The two downstairs guest rooms also share one bath. The hearty country breakfast of juice, farm-fresh eggs in omelettes with fresh herbs, homemade muffins, and more is served in the large country kitchen with views of the pond. Guests at the ranch may watch deer from the living room with its cozy fireplace or take a leisurely walk to the ocean.

Big River Lodge, Mendocino

Big River Lodge—The Stanford Inn by the Sea

P.O. Box 487, Mendocino, CA 95460
Phone: (707) 937-5615
Key: Inn; 23 units; Expensive-Del.; Smoking OK; Children OK;
Credit cards

This lodge on a hillside overlooking the town and the ocean is surrounded by forests and meadows. The spacious guest rooms, uniquely decorated in country antiques, flowers, and art, feature color TV, private entrances and baths, and wood-burning fireplaces or Franklin stoves. The morning breakfast includes special coffee cakes, juices, fruit, and champagne. A carafe of wine awaits guests in each room. The inn is proud of its flower and vegetable gardens, and guests enjoy the friendly llamas that graze nearby.

Blue Heron Inn

P.O. Box 1142, 390 Kasten Street, Mendocino, CA 95460
Phone: (707) 937-4323
Key: Inn; 3 units; Inexpensive-Mod.; Smoking OK; No children;
No credit cards

This b&b in the village offers beautiful ocean views from all rooms. Guest rooms abound in New England–style charm with antiques, down comforters, and feather pillows. Breakfast at the inn brings freshly squeezed orange juice or fresh strawberries, hot croissants or fresh coffee cake, and a special "chocolate moosse" coffee. A small café on the premises tempts "sweet tooths" and serves soup, sandwiches, and salads.

Brewery Gulch Inn

9350 Coast Highway One, Mendocino, CA 95460
Phone: (707) 937-4752
Key: Inn; 5 units; Moderate; No smoking; No children; Credit cards

This 1860s-built white farmhouse on two flower- and tree-filled acres is serenely bordered by pastures, forests, and the rugged coast of the Pacific Ocean. Paths wander through the flower gardens on the old farm, which was once a dairy as well as a beer-brewing operation. The quiet interiors of the inn are filled with Victorian decor; all five guest rooms offer a country warmth with queen-size beds, homemade quilts, and down pillows. Two rooms boast fireplaces, and all of the guest accommodations grant peaceful views, some of which include the ocean. A full country breakfast of such delicacies as Spanish eggs and fried apples or cheese blintzes with ham and blueberries is served at the guest's convenience either in the common room or in the garden.

The Headlands Inn

P.O. Box 132, Howard and Albion streets, Mendocino, CA 95460
Phone: (707) 937-4431

Key: Inn/Cottage; 5 units; Moderate-Exp.; No smoking; No children; No credit cards

This inn, with its spectacular white-water ocean views, was originally built in 1868 as the town's barbershop and then moved and expanded in later years. Restoration has preserved its charm and added present-day comforts. The five guest accommodations each feature a queen- or king-size bed, village or ocean views, private bath, and wood-burning fireplace (one unit offers an old-fashioned parlor stove on a raised hearth). Guests may relax in two parlors. The full breakfast consists of fresh fruit, two home-baked breads or muffins, a hot entree, and beverage.

Joshua Grindle Inn, Mendocino

Joshua Grindle Inn

P.O. Box 647, 44800 Little Lake, Mendocino, CA 95460
Phone: (707) 937-4143
Key: Inn/Cottage; 10 units; Moderate; Smoking OK; No children under 13; No credit cards

This 1879 home, within walking distance of shops and the beach, is on two acres and offers views of the village, bay, and ocean. Guest rooms, each with private bath, are light and airy and are decorated in a New England–country motif with selected antiques. In addition to the inn's accommodations, two guest rooms are located in a cottage and three are in a water-tower building. Many rooms boast ocean views, and some have a fireplace. A breakfast is served each morning at the pine harvest table in the dining room.

MacCallum House

P.O. Box 206, 45020 Albion Street, Mendocino, CA 95460
Phone: (707) 937-0289
Key: Inn/Cottages; 21 units; Inexpensive-Mod.; Smoking OK; Children OK; Credit cards

The large house with gardens was built in 1882. The inn now offers guest accommodations, in the main house and in several buildings on the grounds, as well as a restaurant and bar. Fireplaces, original Tiffany lamps, Persian rugs, period photos, and antiques create a nostalgic feeling in all of the cheerful guest rooms. Separate accommodations are found in the converted carriage house, water tower with split-level lodging, child's playhouse nestled in a bed of geraniums, and barn; many feature Franklin stoves. A continental breakfast is included in the stay.

Mendocino Hotel & Garden Cottages

P.O. Box 587, 45080 Main Street, Mendocino, CA 95460
Phone: (707) 937-0511
Key: Inn/Hotel/Cottages; 51 units; Inexpensive-Del.; Smoking OK; Children OK; Credit cards

The historic hotel, established in 1878, offers elegantly restored lodging, a restaurant, and a lounge overlooking Mendocino Bay. Four cottages have been added in the English garden overlooking the Pacific Ocean. The guest rooms are furnished in Victorian decor with four-poster and brass beds, armoires, and assorted an-

Mendocino Hotel & Garden Cottages, Mendocino

tiques; many rooms boast a balcony, fireplace, or marble bath. Extras at the inn include telephones, televisions, and turn-down service each night. Breakfast, lunch, and dinner are served daily in the hotel's intimate dining rooms.

Mendocino Village Inn

P.O. Box 626, 44860 Main Street, Mendocino, CA 95460
Phone: (707) 937-0246
Key: Inn; 12 units; Inexpensive-Mod.; Limited smoking; No children under 10; Credit cards

Originally built as a doctor's residence in 1882, the home belonged to three more doctors and their families and thus received the appropriate nickname of "the house of doctors." The interiors of the inn are a pleasant blend of Victorian and country decor. The twelve guest accommodations are located upstairs, downstairs, and in the attic. The two attic rooms share a bath on the second floor; all remaining rooms have private baths. Many of the guest rooms grant ocean views, and some offer fireplaces. The full gourmet breakfast varies each day with specialties such as herbed cheesecake or blue cornmeal pancakes. The inn hosts an evening wine hour.

49

1021 Main Street Guest House

P.O. Box 803, Mendocino, CA 95460
Phone: (707) 937-5150
Key: Inn/Cottages; 6 units, Expensive; Smoking OK; No children;
No credit cards

Built by shipwrights around 1861, this farmhouse with barn
and outbuildings overlooking Jackson State Forest, Big River
Beach, Mendocino Bay, and the Pacific affords spectacular views
in all directions. The informal inn offers individual rooms in the
house, all with shared bath, wash basins, and views. An attic suite
features a king-size bed in a loft as well as a skylight and leaded-
glass windows. Cottages offer iron fireplaces and kitchen facilities. Guests are treated to a full breakfast and an ocean-view hot
tub/Jacuzzi.

Sea Gull Inn

P.O. Box 317, Mendocino, CA 95460
Phone: (707) 937-5204
Key: Inn; 9 units; Inexpensive-Mod.; Limited smoking; Children
OK; No credit cards

This 100-year-old original residence, within walking distance
to town, became an inn in the 1960s. A garden lush in fuschias
and boasting a century-old rosemary bush surrounds the quaint
inn, which offers nine guest accommodations, a restaurant, and
cellar bar. The neat guest rooms boast private baths and views of
the headland and ocean. A generous continental breakfast is included in the stay. Lunches and dinners are served in the Sea Gull
Restaurant.

Sea Rock

P.O. Box 286, 11101 N. Lansing, Mendocino, CA 95460
Phone: (707) 937-5517
Key: Inn/Cottages; 16 units; Moderate-Exp.; Smoking OK; Chil-
dren OK; Credit cards

Originally a trailer court, this b&b on a seventy-foot cliff with spectacular white-water views now offers individual cabins set amidst a cypress grove. Along with views of the Mendocino headlands, the blue-gray cabins with white trim offer private flower gardens, fireplaces, color cable TV, brewed in-room coffee, and some antiques and kitchens. The continental breakfast is delivered to the rooms at 8:00 A.M. Guests enjoy a lawn area and a private beach and cove, where they may wade through tidal pools, collect shells, or fish for abalone

Whitegate Inn, Mendocino

Whitegate Inn

P.O. Box 150, 499 Howard Street, Mendocino, CA 95460
Phone: (707) 937-4892
Key: Inn; 6 units; Moderate; Limited smoking; No children under 14; No credit cards

The 1880 home, overlooking the town park, has been refurbished and is decorated totally in antiques. The guest rooms all feature their own sitting areas, and many have private baths and fireplaces. Fruit and homemade breads or waffles greet guests in the dining room each morning; a parlor decanter of wine is shared in the early evening.

51

Glendeven

8221 N. Highway One, Little River, CA 95456
Phone: (707) 937-0083
Key: Inn; 10 units; Moderate-Exp.; Limited smoking, Children on approval; Credit cards

This small inn within an 1867-built, Maine-style farmhouse overlooks meadows and the bay. Guest rooms, mainly with private baths, are decorated in antiques, contemporary artwork, and exciting colors, and some boast a fireplace. A brick terrace, gardens, and sitting room provide relaxation. The spacious sitting area with fireplace and baby grand piano is the locale of the morning breakfast unless in-room service is requested.

Heritage House

5200 Highway One, Little River, CA 95456
Phone: (707) 937-5885
Key: Inn/Cottages; 67 units; Expensive-Del.; Smoking OK; Children OK; No credit cards

This country inn expands on the b&b concept by serving a full breakfast and a six-course dinner along with the overnight stay. The Maine-style complex perched on the dramatic coastline consists of an 1877 farmhouse (now office), with dining room, kitchen, and a handful of guest rooms, and several guest cottages that blend in with the landscape. Accommodations are furnished with local historical pieces, and all quarters enjoy beautiful views and peaceful surroundings.

The Victorian Farmhouse

P.O. Box 357, 7001 N. Highway One, Little River, CA 95456
Phone: (707) 937-0697
Key: Inn; 6 units; Moderate; Smoking OK; No children under 11; No credit cards

An apple orchard, flower gardens, School House Creek, and nearby Buckhorn Cove offer relaxation and recreation to this 1877 farmhouse's guests. Guest rooms all have king- or queen-size beds covered with quilts from the innkeeper's collection, private baths, and period antiques; two rooms boast a fireplace. Upstairs rooms offer ocean views. Breakfast is brought to the room each morning, and for evening enjoyment sherry is placed in the parlor, which has a bay window and fireplace.

Fensalden

P.O. Box 99, 33810 Navarro Ridge Road, Albion, CA 95410
Phone: (707) 937-4042
Key: Inn; 12 units; Moderate-Exp.; No smoking; No children under 11; Credit cards

Built originally in the 1860s as a stagecoach stop and tavern and later used as a farmhouse until its recent renovation to a b&b, this inn is situated on twenty acres of meadow land sweeping down to the rugged coast below. The inn's name translates appropriately to "land of the mist and sea." The interiors of the b&b are a pleasant melding of antique and traditional decor punctuated with fine art. Special touches in the guest rooms, all with private baths, include handmade pottery sinks, cozy down-filled quilts, and impressive ocean and countryside views. Homebaked breads and muffins, fruit, freshly squeezed juice, and coffee or tea are served in the "Tavern Room," the parlor, or in the privacy of your room. Complimentary wine and hors d'oeuvres are served at sunset in this tranquil and inspiring spot.

Oak Knoll Bed & Breakfast

P.O. Box 412, 858 Sanel Drive, Ukiah, CA 95482
Phone: (707) 468-5646
Key: Home; 2 units; Inexpensive; No smoking; No children; No credit cards

This contemporary redwood-and-glass home sits on a knoll studded with oak trees and enjoys views of the hills, valley, and vineyards on all sides. A 3,000-square-foot deck with solar spa, Jacuzzi, and tables and chairs is the site of the morning meal. Both guest accommodations feature a queen-size bed and fresh flowers and share a bath and adjacent sitting room with games and color television. The house is decorated in wallcoverings, chandeliers, and Oriental rugs; guests may enjoy fireside relaxation in either the family room, with its forty-inch-screen television, or the living room, with its piano. Breakfast served on fine china includes fruit, juice, homemade breads, and pastries; eggs and bacon are available. Wine and cheese are offered in the evening.

Sanford House

306 South Pine Street, Ukiah, CA 95482
Phone: (707) 462-1653
Key: Inn; 5 units; Moderate; Limited smoking; No children under 13; No credit cards

In the heart of the Mendocino wine country is this 1904-built Queen Anne–Victorian home that was the residence of Senator John Sanford and his family until 1944. A rare bird's-eye-maple fireplace warms the antique-filled parlor of the inn. Also, the library is a popular gathering spot with its cozy window seat. The five individually decorated guest rooms, all named after presidents who served between 1904 and 1928, are located upstairs and feature quaint wallpaper prints, fresh flowers, antique decor, and private baths. A chilled bottle of local wine is brought to the room upon your arrival. The complimentary continental breakfast is served either in the dining room on fine china and crystal or in the privacy of your room. Guests are encouraged to relax in the backyard gazebo or on the large porch furnished with nostalgic wicker furniture.

Elk Cove Inn

6300 S. Highway One, P.O. Box 367, Elk, CA 95432
Phone: (707) 877-3321
Key: Inn/Guesthouses; 9 units; Moderate-Exp.; No smoking; No children under 9; No credit cards

Elk Cove Inn, Elk

This early 1880s Victorian house, cabin, and guest house provide dramatic views of the rocky coast and surf. Guest accommodations in the main building and guest houses are decorated in antiques with lots of flowers, plants, and hand-embroidered linens. Guests enjoy a secluded beach, numerous scenic trails, a living room with fireplace, and a large library. French and German specialties delight guests, whose lodging includes daily breakfast and both breakfast and dinner on Saturday.

Green Dolphin Inn

6145 S. Highway One, P.O. Box 132, Elk, CA 95432
Phone: (707) 877-3342
Key: Inn/Guesthouse; 3 units; Expensive; Smoking OK; No children; No credit cards

This small inn, commanding spectacular views of the ocean and boulders off the coast, offers one room in the main house and guest accommodations on both floors of an adjacent carriage house. All accommodations boast private baths and country-antique furnishings. The house provides a common area and a full library with massive fireplace. The complete breakfast, served with sea views in the upstairs dining room, is delightfully different each day. Guests also enjoy a hot tub.

Greenwood Lodge

P.O. Box 172, 5910 S. Highway One, Elk, CA 95432
Phone: (707) 877-3422
Key: Inn/Cottages; 7 units; Moderate-Exp.; No smoking; No children under 10; No credit cards

This turn-of-the-century lodge offers private, cozy cottages with views of the ocean and harbor or with the intimacy of fragrant flower gardens. The individual cottages are uniquely decorated and furnished with brass beds, comforters, armoires, claw-foot bathtubs, leaded and stained-glass windows, wood-burning stoves, and private baths. Some units feature sitting rooms or decks overlooking the ocean. A generous breakfast of local fruit juices, fruit, homemade muffins, coffee cakes or eggs, and locally blended coffee is brought to the cottages each morning.

Harbor House, Elk

Harbor House

5600 S. Highway One, P.O. Box 369, Elk, CA 95432
Phone: (707) 877-3203
Key: Inn/Cottages; 10 units; Expensive-Del.; Limited smoking; No children; No credit cards

The entirely redwood-constructed main building of the 1916 inn sits on a bluff overlooking a once-busy lumber port. The tranquil setting offers accommodations in the redwood structure as well as in adjacent cottages. All guest quarters host private baths and either fireplaces or Franklin stoves and have private-beach rights. Guests at the small inn are served both breakfast and dinner in the ocean-view dining room as a part of the overnight stay, making the b&b a moderate splurge.

Anderson Creek Inn

P.O. Box 217, 12050 Anderson Valley Way, Boonville, CA 95415
Phone: (707) 895-3091
Key: Home; 4 units; Moderate-Exp.; Limited smoking; No children under 9; Credit cards

This sprawling ranch house on thirty-seven acres of land with two streams is nestled deep within Anderson Valley and is surrounded by mountains and nature. Each of the spacious guest rooms at this ranch b&b has its own serene view, color TV, and unique antique decor with both shared- and private-bath accommodations available. Guests here enjoy a game room with pool table, an exercise room, an indoor spa, and a twenty-by-forty-foot in-ground pool surrounded by a large deck. The flower-filled "breakfast" garden is the site of morning waffles, bacon, eggs, fruit, juice, and hot farm-style coffee at this quiet retreat. Weekly rates are available, and free shuttle service is provided to and from the nearby airport.

Toll House Inn

P.O. Box 268, 15301 Highway 253, Boonville, CA 95415
Phone: (707) 895-3630
Key: Inn; 4 units; Inexpensive-Mod.; Smoking OK; No children under 12; No credit cards

A hot tub, sun deck, croquet, horseshoes, and nearby stables provide recreation for guests in this private and secluded resort. Two guest rooms and two suites, the latter with fireplaces and private baths, come with a full country breakfast and a complimentary bottle of wine. Dinners are prepared with advance warning, and the seclusion of the outside areas make this a popular site for miniretreats.

Philo Pottery Inn, Philo

Philo Pottery Inn

P.O. Box 166, 8550 Route 128, Philo, CA 95466
Phone: (707) 895-3069
Key: Inn; 5 units; Moderate; No smoking; No children under 9;
No credit cards

This historic house, built entirely of redwood, was a late-1800s stagecoach stop. The inn, with its views of the surrounding hills, is nestled in a lush valley and is fronted by a large English flower garden. A vegetable garden sits alongside the house, and to the rear of the inn is a pottery studio and gallery open to guests. A living room with piano and library is for guests' use. Guest rooms feature antique furnishings and touches such as armoires, iron and brass beds, claw-foot tubs, and Laura Ashley prints, as well as private decks, stained-glass windows, and floor tiles made in the inn's own pottery studio. The homemade, New England–farmhouse-style breakfast of orange juice, freshly ground coffee, teas, fruit breads, and croissants with homemade preserves, yogurt, and fresh fruit is served in the dining room. A complimentary bottle of wine also is included in the stay.

The Old Milano Hotel

38300 Highway One, Gualala, CA 95445
Phone: (707) 884-3256

Key: Inn/Cottages; 9 units; Moderate-Del.; No smoking; No children under 18; Credit cards

This hotel, which began as a 1905 rest stop and pub alongside the railroad, has been refurbished throughout. Accommodations include six guest rooms and two baths upstairs with ocean or garden views, a suite with a hand-painted canopy bed, and two vine-covered cottages with kitchens, baths, sitting areas, and pot-belly stoves. Guests enjoy the hotel's gardens and hot tub, perched above a cove. The complimentary continental breakfast consists of home-baked breads, a fresh fruit dish, and locally roasted coffee. The inn's chef offers gourmet dinners Thursday through Monday.

St. Orres

P.O. Box 523, Gualala, CA 95445
Phone: (707) 884-3303
Key: Inn/Cottages; 18 units; Moderate-Del.; Smoking OK; Children, cottages only; Credit cards

Inspired by Russian architecture and constructed of 100-year-old timbers, the inn with restaurant is a unique b&b offering. Accommodations include eight rooms in the inn, each with double bed and handmade quilt and some with stained-glass windows and balconies, as well as a cabin and nine cottages offering kitchens, wood-burning stoves, and decks. A continental breakfast is included, and dinner is available in the restaurant. The inn has recently added a creek-side spa area.

Whale Watch

35100 Highway One, Gualala, CA 95445
Phone: (707) 884-3667
Key: Inn; 18 units; Expensive-Del.; Limited smoking; No children; Credit cards

Located on two cliff-side acres overlooking Anchor Bay with breathtaking views of the Mendocino coastline is this contemporary inn with beach access. Five building compose the inn and offer eighteen unique guest accommodations that feature such varied amenities as fireplaces, skylights, queen-size beds, down comforters, whirlpool tubs, two-story units, fully equipped kitchens, sitting areas, private decks, and private baths. Guests enjoy a large lounge with ocean views and a generous continental breakfast served in the room; wine is available.

The Estate

13555 Highway 116, Guerneville, CA 95446
Phone: (707) 869-9093
Key: Inn; 10 units; Moderate-Exp.; Smoking OK; No children; Credit cards

The three-story, Mission Revival country home, a Sonoma County Historical Landmark, sits on six acres with redwood groves, gardens, and apple orchards; the grounds feature a large, terraced heated pool and spa. The 1922-built stucco structure with tile roof offers ten guest rooms with private baths, antique decor, and queen beds. Special touches include freshly cut flowers, imported soaps and toiletries, down pillows and comforters, remote color television, telephones, and evening turn-down service with chocolates. Common rooms at the inn include a solarium with bay-window views, a "Great Room," a "Breakfast Room," and a large, formal dining room with French doors opening on the pool and gardens. The lower level of the inn contains a sitting room and library with balcony and covered porch. The full breakfast of juice, French roast coffee, and specialties such as sausages and apple-stuffed French toast with local apple syrup is served in the solarium, breakfast or main dining rooms, or by the pool. Complimentary wine is offered each evening; dinner is available on arrangement. The Estate often hosts chamber-music concerts and art exhibits.

Ridenhour Ranch House Inn

12850 River Road, Guerneville, CA 95446
Phone: (707) 887-1033
Key: Inn; 8 units; Moderate; Limited smoking; No children under 11; Credit cards

This eleven-room country house built at the turn of the century is within walking distance of the Korbel Winery's champagne cellars. The carefully restored inn offers guest rooms decorated individually in country English and American antiques with quilts, flowers, plants, and decanters of wine. Guests may stroll under the redwoods, soak in the hot tub, or relax in front of the comfortable living room's fireplace. The country kitchen, formal dining room, or garden terrace provides the setting for the full, creative breakfast by the owner/chef. The inn is closed January 2 through mid-February.

Santa Nella House

12130 Highway 116, Guerneville, CA 95446
Phone: 869-9488
Key: Home; 4 units; Moderate; No smoking; No children; Credit cards

Formerly the winemaster's residence of the circa-1880 Santa Nella Winery, this b&b offers guests overnight lodging along with a full champagne breakfast. The house sits among the redwoods with the Korbel vineyard in view and Pocket Creek passing through the frontage. The guest rooms boast Victorian decor, private baths, and plush red carpeting; two rooms have fireplaces. Guests may relax in the parlor with its wood-burning fireplace or sun on the large wraparound veranda.

The House of a Thousand Flowers

P.O. Box 369, Monte Rio, CA 95462
Phone: (707) 632-5571
Key: Home; 2 units; Moderate; No smoking; Children on approval; No credit cards

The 1967 house on a bluff overlooks the Russian River and is surrounded by flowering trees and gardens and sunny decks. The comfortably furnished guest rooms each have a private entrance and impressive forest and valley views. Guests enjoy a warm spa on the outside, enclosed deck plus a large living room, with fireplace and concert grand piano, stocked with books and music. Coffee is served in-room each morning, and a full breakfast of omelettes, bread, and fruit is offered in the dining room. A library-music room and greenhouse sitting room have recently been added.

Timberhill Resort

35755 Hauser Bridge Road, Cazadero, CA 95421
Phone: (707) 847-3258
Key: Inn/Cottages; 10 units; Deluxe; Limited smoking; No children; Credit cards

This country ranch and tennis resort surrounded by 6,000 acres of state parkland offers ten private cedar cottages for two and includes all three gourmet meals in the stay. The newly constructed cottages with redwood decks sit on former Kashia Pomo Indian ground now home to horses and llamas, a pond with wild ducks, and spring wildflowers. Each carefully appointed cottage boasts a romantic wood-burning fireplace, handmade quilt, and tiled bath. Special amenities include a forty-foot pool, a Jacuzzi with views of the hills, and world-class tennis courts. Trays of homemade breads, fruit, juice, and beverages are served in each cottage in the morning, and lunch may be enjoyed poolside, on one of the main decks, in the lodge dining room, or elsewhere by picnic basket. The intimate main lodge is the locale of the fireside dinner that features six courses with a generous choice of entrees and homemade desserts. Each cottage boasts its own fully stocked refrigerator, and beverages are offered by the pool and at the tennis courts throughout the day.

Murphy's Jenner by the Sea

P.O. Box 69, 10400 Coast Highway One, Jenner, CA 95450
Phone: (707) 865-2377
Key: Inn/Cottage; 13 units; Moderate-Exp.; Smoking OK; No children under 13; Credit cards

This b&b, consisting of three complete houses of suites and rooms, offers country, river, and ocean views. Situated at the meeting point of the Russian River and the Pacific, the inn's accommodations include suites with living room, kitchen, bedroom, private bath, and woodstove and guest rooms with private bath, antiques, handmade quilts, and plants. A complimentary full breakfast is served in the salon or main dining room, where continental dinner cuisine and entertainment also are offered.

Green Apple Inn

520 Bohemian Highway, Freestone, CA 95472
Phone: (707) 874-2526
Key: Inn; 4 units; Moderate; No smoking; Children on approval; Credit cards

This New England–style farmhouse built in 1862 is located on five acres in a designated historic area. The inn is furnished with family pieces from the 1700s, and the cheery rooms look out on the countryside. Guests enjoy a parlor with fireplace and a full breakfast. Recreation is all close by, with many fine restaurants, family wineries, biking, and canoeing available in this spot near the Russian River.

CALIFORNIA WINE COUNTRY

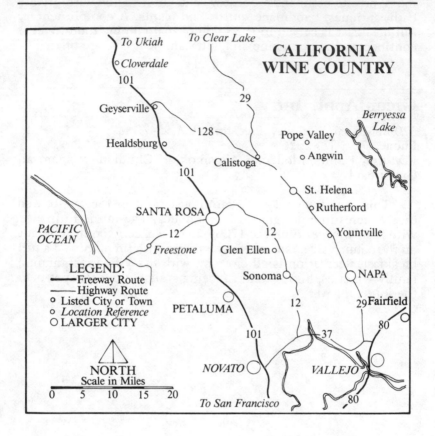

Endless fields of grapes that stretch out to picturesque moun-tain slopes, historic town squares, country roads dotted with quiet communities, natural hot springs, and renowned wineries all define the Wine Country of the Napa and Sonoma valleys and the Russian River. Add the popular sport of ballooning to vineyard vistas, ideal picnic scenery, lakes, and spas, and this area becomes a natural haven for travelers. This by far is the most popular region for bed & breakfasts, and it is no wonder, what with the perfect settings that abound: ranches, wineries, and quiet Victo-rian towns. The history of the area is apparent in the town of Sonoma, with its plaza and Mission, and in Yountville's unusual shopping complex reminiscent of its winery origins, vintage 1870. Calistoga still offers mud baths and mineral-spring spas and the nearby Old Faithful Geyser with its regular eruptions. Country serenity, wine picnicking, and gracious bed & breakfast stops throughout—Wine Country, a relaxing and most pleasurable vacation spot.

Vintage Towers Inn

302 N. Main Street, Cloverdale, CA 95425
Phone: (707) 894-4535
Key: Inn; 8 units; Inexpensive-Mod.; No smoking; No children under 10; Credit cards

The Queen Anne–Victorian mansion is listed on the Na-tional Register of Historic Places. The mansion grounds offer many sitting areas, a rose garden, and an old-fashioned gazebo. Accommodations at the inn include three tower suites: one round, one square, and one octagonal; the decor is all turn of the century. The morning meal is served in the formal dining room, on the veranda, or in the gazebo. Afternoon refreshments, bicy-cles, airport pickup service, and family hospitality are all in-cluded at this inn located six blocks from the Russian River.

Ye Olde Shelford House, Cloverdale

Ye Olde Shelford House

29955 River Road, Cloverdale, CA 95425
Phone: (707) 894-5956
Key: Inn; 3 units; Moderate; No smoking; No children under 11;
Credit cards

Bordering on acres of vineyards is this late-1800s home near the Russian River. The completely restored interiors of this intimate b&b feature antiques, cozy window seats, quaint wallcoverings (on the ceilings, too), and several relaxing niches including an outside wraparound porch, a game room, a parlor, an upstairs sitting room, and a hot tub. Those wanting more activity may borrow the inn's "bicycle built for two" or tubes to meander down the river. The three guest rooms offer homemade quilts, antiques, and fresh flowers and plants. A full homemade breakfast is included in the stay, and a special champagne brunch is offered on Sundays. Guests may help themselves to refreshments and old-fashioned oatmeal cookies from the kitchen. Reservations are advised for the inn's popular "Surrey & Sip" horse-drawn surrey rides to the wineries.

Campbell Ranch Inn

1475 Canyon Road, Geyservile, CA 95441
Phone: (707) 857-3476
Key: Home; 4 units; Moderate; No smoking; No children; No credit cards

This hilltop, contemporary home looks out onto vineyards and the ranch's own colorful flower gardens. This thirty-five acre "miniresort" treats guests to tennis, swimming, hiking, Ping-Pong, a hot tub, and bikes, as well as a living-room fireplace. The spacious rooms feature king- or queen-size beds, balconies, fresh flowers, and fruit. Besides the full gourmet breakfast, fresh pie and coffee are offered before bedtime, and unlimited iced tea and lemonade are served poolside.

The Hope-Bosworth House

P.O. Box 42, 21238 Geyserville Avenue, Geyserville, CA 95441
Phone: (707) 857-3356
Key: Inn; 5 units; Inexpensive-Mod.; No smoking; Children on approval; Credit cards

This 1904 Victorian home was earlier called the "Palms" because of the many palm trees once lining the street. Two seventy-foot trees remain. All of the guest rooms are decorated in wallpapers, antique light fixtures, and period antiques. A formal dining room is the site of the morning full country breakfast featuring the innkeeper's prize-winning coffee cake, and wine is offered in the parlor each day. Guests at the inn enjoy a colorful, fragrant Victorian garden and use of the swimming pool.

The Hope-Merrill House

P.O. Box 42, 21253 Geyserville Avenue, Geyserville, CA 95441
Phone: (707) 857-3356
Key: Inn; 5 units; Moderate; No smoking; Children on approval; Credit cards

The 1885 home was restored completely and carefully in 1980 with authentic wallcoverings and woodwork and the original Lincrusta-Walton wainscoting. Guests may relax with a glass of wine on the wraparound porch or in the parlor. A country breakfast featuring homemade breads, fresh fruit, and eggs is served in the dining room. Dinners are available upon prearrangment. Individually decorated guest rooms at the inn feature such varied touches as a fireplace, bay-window views, unusual antiques, Bradbury wallpapers, and antique bath fixtures in the all-private baths that include two whirlpool tubs. The inn offers a unique wine tour called Stage-a-Picnic that visits three wineries via a 100-year-old stage drawn by two Belgian horses and also includes a gourmet picnic. Guests enjoy a garden swimming pool and a gazebo in the vineyards.

Isis Oasis

20889 Geyserville Avenue, Geyserville, CA 95441
Phone: (707) 857-3524
Key: Inn; 12 units; Moderate; Smoking OK; Children by arrangement; Credit cards

This eight-acre lodge and cultural center contains four historic buildings, minizoo, swimming pool, spa, sauna, a dinner theater, and a wilderness area. A chalet lodge houses the dozen guest rooms and a large lounge with fireplace and bay-window views. The stay at this rustic b&b includes complimentary wine upon arrival and an ample country breakfast.

Belle de Jour Farm

16276 Healdsburg Avenue, Healdsburg, CA 95448
Phone: (707) 433-7892
Key: Inn/Cottages; 5 units; Moderate; No smoking; No children; Credit cards

This garden b&b offers fresh white cottages nestled in six private acres with panoramic views of the countryside. One guest accommodation is located in the farmhouse, an 1873-built Italianate home, and shares a bath. The other guest rooms, decorated in antiques, are situated in separate cottages of newer vintage and offer private baths and queen- or king-size beds. Special details in some of the accommodations include wood stoves, a fireplace, oversized showers, and one whirlpool tub for two. A sumptuous breakfast is included in the stay; picnic baskets and dinner service are available on arrangement, as is winery touring via vintage cars.

Camellia Inn

211 North Street, Healdsburg, CA 95448
Phone: (707) 433-8182
Key: Inn; 7 units; Inexpensive-Mod.; No smoking; Children on approval; Credit cards

Built in 1869, this Italianate–Victorian townhouse is just two blocks from the town plaza. The guest rooms are decorated in antiques, inlaid hardwood floors, chandeliers, and oriental rugs; four rooms feature private entrances and baths. Guests are encouraged to enjoy the villa-styled swimming pool and the double parlors with twin marble fireplaces and ceiling medallions. The breakfast of fresh fruit, eggs, nut breads, and juice is served in the dining room, and sherry is available in the parlors.

Camellia Inn, Healdsburg

Grape Leaf Inn

539 Johnson Street, Healdsburg, CA 95448
Phone: (707) 433-8140
Key: Inn/Cottages; 8 units; Moderate-Exp.; No smoking; No children under 10; Credit cards

This 1902 Queen Anne–Victorian home has been completely restored and offers seven guest accommodations, all with private baths, skylight roofs, and antiques. Four of the guest rooms and suites feature tiled whirlpool tubs. Guests read, play games, or just relax in a parlor with antiques and a living room/dining room with fireplace and comfortable seating. A full breakfast featuring egg dishes and homebaked breads is served in the dining room. Wine and cheeses are offered in the evening.

The Haydon House

321 Haydon Street, Healdsburg, CA 95448
Phone: (707) 433-5228
Key: Inn/Cottage; 8 units; Moderate-Exp.; No smoking; No children under 10; Credit cards

A short walk from the Russian River and downtown shops takes you to this lovely Queen Anne–Victorian home in a quiet

The Haydon House, Healdsburg

residential area. The one-time convent has been meticulously restored to its 1912 vintage and dons such period detailing as picture moldings, chair rails and baseboards, stenciling, and wallpapering. The light and airy rooms are furnished in antiques, handmade rugs, lace curtains, and pastels. The cheerful guest rooms feature a favorite of honeymooners, the "Attic Suite" with skylights, and all are individually decorated in French and American antique, Dhurrie Rugs, Laura Ashley prints, and custom-made down comforters. Claw-foot tubs grace several of the rooms. Complimentary wine is served on the living-room sideboard, and a bountiful breakfast featuring frittatas is offered in the large dining room each morning. Two accommodations are located in a separate Victorian-style cottage that boasts pine floors, double whirlpool tubs with skylights, and romantic laces.

Healdsburg Inn on the Plaza

P.O. Box 1196, 116 Matheson Street, Healdsburg, CA 95448
Phone: (707) 433-6991
Key: Inn; 9 units; Moderate-Exp.; Limited smoking; No children under 8; Credit cards

This renovated 1900-built Wells Fargo building hosts quaint shops and a guest lobby below and attractive b&b guest rooms above. Rooms at the inn feature huge skylights, bay windows,

71

pressed wood paneling, and Victorian and Eastlake decor. Three guest rooms boast fireplaces, and all accommodations have private baths. The gingerbread-adorned brick building looks over the historic plaza and offers an all-weather solarium and roof garden for socializing. A full breakfast with home-baked breads and a hot entree is served in the solarium. Wine and popcorn are offered in the evening.

L'auberge du Sans-Souci, Healdsburg

L'auberge du Sans-Souci

25 West Grant, Healdsburg, CA 95448
Phone: (707) 431-1110
Key: Inn; 5 units; Moderate; Limited smoking; No children; Credit cards

Its name translated from the French as "an inn of the carefree or relaxed," this European-feeling b&b is housed in a finely restored redwood Victorian nestled among spruce, cedar, and redwood trees. The French innkeeper serves her b&b guests a breakfast of croissants hot from the oven along with homemade preserves and coffee on the porch overlooking the old garden. The 1902 residence's interiors include rooms filled with fine European antiques and five guest rooms with queen-size beds, down comforters, newly tiled bathrooms, and air conditioning. After a day of touring, guests are invited to a tasting of Sonoma County wines in the garden.

Madrona Manor

P.O. Box 818, 1001 Westside Road, Healdsburg, CA 95448
Phone: (707) 433-4231/433-4433
Key: Inn/Hotel; 20 units; Moderate-Del.; Smoking OK; Children OK; Credit cards

This lavish 1881 Victorian mansion is surrounded by eight acres of wooded and landscaped grounds. Today, the ornate hotel and gourmet restaurant offer guest rooms and suites decorated in antiques, Persian carpets, and hand-carved rosewood. All rooms boast air conditioning and private baths. The acclaimed restaurant at the mansion has an extensive wine list and serves dinners nightly as well as Sunday brunch.

The Raford House, Healdsburg

The Raford House

10630 Wohler Road, Healdsburg, CA 95448
Phone: (707) 887-9573
Key: Inn; 7 units; Moderate; No smoking; Children on approval; Credit cards

This 1880s home, formerly the Wohler Ranch, is a beautifully restored Victorian farmhouse with thirteen rooms and six

73

baths surrounded by vineyards. The seven guest rooms are decorated in period pieces; two have working fireplaces, and most offer private baths. A large front porch overlooks the vineyards and orchards as well as the inn's rose bushes, which number more than one hundred. A light breakfast of rolls, breads, and juice is served in the dining room or on the front porch.

Big Canyon Inn

P.O. Box 1311, Lower Lake, CA,
11750 Big Canyon Road, Middletown, CA 95457
Phone: (707) 928-5631
Key: Home; 2 units; Inexpensive; No smoking; Children OK; No credit cards

This secluded mountain cabin on twelve acres of pines and oaks is surrounded by recreational opportunities ranging from wildflower viewing in spring to winetasting to boating on nearby Clear Lake. Guests are accommodated in a suite with private porch, entrance, and bath as well as kitchenette, air conditioning, and cozy woodstove. Accommodations also boast a nice front-porch view overlooking the valley. A continental breakfast of pastry and fruit is served each morning. As a special service, private pilots flying into local Hoberg Airport and staying at the inn will be picked up by the hosts.

Brannan Cottage Inn

109 Wapoo Avenue, Calistoga, CA 94515
Phone: (707) 942-4200
Key: Inn; 6 units; Moderate-Exp.; Smoking OK; Children OK; Credit cards

This 1860 cottage inn with graceful arches, gingerbread, and original palm tree is the last remaining Sam Brannan-built cottage at his "Calistoga Hot Springs Resort" and is listed on the National Register of Historic Places. The carefully restored structure is decorated Victorian country style with light oak floors, pine furnishings, and white wicker. The six guest rooms and suites boast the original hand-done flower stenciling as well as private baths and entrances, queen-size beds, down comforters, ceiling fans, and air conditioning. The elegant parlor is furnished in rose and gray with a grapevine stencil border, etched oval window, cozy fireplace, and sherry and port. Afternoon tea is served fireside in cool weather. The full breakfast is served in the enclosed court-yard under the lemon trees on sunny mornings. The tranquil cottage inn is surrounded by lawns and gardens and is within walking distance of Calistoga's hot springs, restaurants, and shops.

Culver's, A Country Inn, Calistoga

Culver's, A Country Inn

1805 Foothill Boulevard, Calistoga, CA 94515
Phone: (707) 942-4535
Key: Inn; 7 units; Moderate; Limited smoking; No children under 13; Credit cards

This gracious, 1875-built Victorian mansion on a hillside with views of the valley has a covered porch overlooking a lawn with shade trees and a garden path leading to a swimming pool, sun deck, and spa. The interior of the inn has a country feel accomplished by light colors, soft wallpapers, antiques, and an oak-paneled fireplace. The individually appointed guest rooms, such as the "Edwardian," are decorated in various vintage decors, and all share baths. A generous continental breakfast is served as well as evening sherry. Guests enjoy a living room with player piano, a library, and a downstairs sauna. Groups occupying the entire inn may arrange for gourmet catered dinners served in the inn's formal dining room.

Foothill House

3037 Foothill Boulevard, Calistoga, CA 94515
Phone: (707) 942-6933
Key: Inn; 3 units; Moderate-Exp.; No smoking; No children under 13; Credit cards

Nestled among the western foothills north of Calistoga is this turn-of-the-century farmhouse surrounded by trees and wildlife. Each room is individually decorated with country antiques, a handmade quilt, and a four-poster bed. All rooms have queen-size beds, private baths and entrances, refrigerators, and fireplaces or stoves as well as air conditioning. The newly completed "Evergreen Suite" offers the same amenities plus a Jacuzzi tub, private garden, and sun deck. An ample continental breakfast is served in the room, on the sun porch, or on the terrace, and guests partake of wine and cheese each evening.

Larkmead Country Inn

1103 Larkmead Lane, Calistoga, CA 94515
Phone: (707) 942-5360
Key: Inn; 4 units; Expensive; Smoking OK; No children; No credit cards

This California Victorian was built as a home for one of the first wine-producing families of Napa Valley. The inn is situated on a quiet country road and surrounded by vineyards and trees. The guest rooms are tastefully furnished with antiques, Persian carpets, and old paintings and are centrally air-conditioned. Breakfast, served in the dining room or on the porches, consists of fresh fruit, brioche, and French rolls.

Mount View Hotel

1457 Lincoln Avenue, Calistoga, CA 94515
Phone: (707) 942-6877
Key: Inn/Hotel; 34 units; Inexpensive-Exp.; Smoking OK; Children OK; Credit cards

This 1917 hotel has been restored in the Art Deco style and is on the National Register of Historic Places. Much of its furniture, lighting, and bath fixtures is original. The Mount View has Fender's, a full service lounge with entertainment nightly and Sunday-afternoon jazz. The dining room serves Napa Valley cuisine at breakfast, lunch, Sunday brunch, and dinner. A full breakfast is included in the stay and served in the privacy of the room. All rooms offer private baths, and guests enjoy nightly turn-down service, a heated pool, and a Jacuzzi.

Scarlett's Country Inn, Calistoga

Scarlett's Country Inn

3918 Silverado Trail, North Calistoga, CA 94515
Phone: (707) 942-6669
Key: Inn/Cottage; 3 units; Moderate-Exp.; Smoking OK; Children OK; Credit cards

This cottage b&b is separate from the main two-story farm-house, and it is located in a quiet canyon off the road. A suite with private bath has a queen-size, wood-carved bed, French country antiques, and claw-foot tub. Two other suites overlooking the vineyards also are available. Guests enjoy a pool and a homemade continental breakfast served under the apple trees by the pool or in the suite.

Trailside Inn

4201 Silverado Trail, Calistoga, CA 94515
Phone: (707) 942-4106
Key: Inn; 2 units; Moderate; Smoking OK; Children OK; No credit cards

This inn has two suites for guests: one attached to the one-story, 1930s farmhouse, the other within the fifty-year-old barn. Both feature an antique, brass double bed in the bedroom; a living room with twin daybeds; and a private entrance, bath, and porch with views of the vineyards. The complete kitchens in each are stocked with homemade fruit bread, orange juice, butter, eggs, fruit, wine, mineral water, and coffee for both breakfast and refreshment time. Each unit will accommodate up to four people; there is no charge for children under 12.

Wine Way Inn

1019 Foothill Boulevard, Highway 29, Calistoga, CA 94515
Phone: (707) 942-0680
Key: Inn/Cottage; 6 units; Moderate; Smoking OK; No children under 10; Credit cards

The inn, built in 1915 as a family home, is located within walking distance of shops yet offers deck views of the mountains and forests of the area. Guest rooms, all with central air conditioning, are furnished in nineteenth-century American and English antiques and are supplied with a decanter of wine and fresh flowers. A separate cottage offers a private bath and spectacular

Wine Way Inn, Calistoga

views. The patio or dining room is the site of morning breakfast. Guests select from homemade pastries, frittatas, fruits, and juices. Guests may enjoy the new hillside gazebo for private moments and intimate breakfasts.

Zinfandel House

1253 Summit Drive, Calistoga, CA 94515
Phone: (707) 942-0733
Key: Home; 2 units; Moderate; No smoking; No children; No credit cards

This home is situated on a wooded hillside overlooking vineyards and the mountains across the valley. The two guest rooms boast private baths, down pillows and comforters, and handmade quilts. Breakfast is served on the deck with majestic views, and wine is offered in late afternoon.

Forest Manor

415 Cold Springs Road, Angwin, CA 94508
Phone: (707) 965-3538
Key: Inn; 3 units; Moderate-Exp.; No smoking; No children under 10; Credit cards

This majestic English Tudor estate on twenty secluded acres is nestled among the hillside forests and vineyards above St. Helena. The manor features massive hand-carved beams, fireplaces, a fifty-three-foot-long pool with Jacuzzi, and spacious suites with private baths, decks, refrigerators, and coffeemakers. One suite offers a private Jacuzzi, fireplace, and king-size bed. The generous continental breakfast may be served fireside in the breakfast room, on the tree-shaded deck, or in the room. Guests enjoy walking trails and nearby tennis.

Ambrose Bierce House

1515 Main Street, St. Helena, CA 94574
Phone: (707) 963-3003
Key: Inn; 2 units; Moderate-Del.; Smoking OK; No children under 13; Credit cards

Vines climb lazily on the 1872-built house that was once the residence of poet, essayist, and witty author Ambrose Bierce. In a residential area with well-tended gardens and lawn, this small b&b inn offers guests a spacious sitting room and bedroom suites named after late-1800s Napa Valley personalities. Each history-filled guest room contains antiques, a queen-size brass bed, Laura Ashley wallpaper, and an armoire. The private bathrooms are Victorian with claw-foot tubs and brass fittings. Italian pastries, fruit, and juice greet guests in the morning; complimentary sherry is offered in the evening.

Bale Mill Inn

3431 N. St. Helena Highway, St. Helena, CA 94574
Phone: (707) 963-4545

Bale Mill Inn, St. Helena

Key: Inn; 5 units; Moderate; Smoking OK; No children under 7; Credit cards

The bottom floor of this country inn contains a rustic antique shop, while the guest rooms share two baths upstairs. Each room is decorated in an individual theme concerning a famous person, such as the "E. Dickinson" room with natural wickers and an antique brass and iron bed. The sitting room features French doors yielding onto views of the valley; it is the site of evening wine. Breakfast offers freshly baked cinnamon bread warming in the antique oven, pastries, and juice.

Bartels Ranch & Country Inn

1200 Conn Valley Road, St. Helena, CA 94574
Phone: (707) 963-4001
Key: Inn; 3 units; Expensive-Del.; Limited smoking; No children under 13; No credit cards

Surrounded by hills, pines, and oaks, the ranch offers peaceful lodging along with a swimming pool and Jacuzzi and recreation room with fireplace, pool, television, and Ping Pong. Decorated in antiques, wicker, and contemporary prints, the guest rooms share a private entrance and deck, and one accommodation offers a private bath. The continental breakfast and evening wine, fruit, and cheese are included.

Chestleson House

1417 Kearney Street, St. Helena, CA 94574
Phone: (707) 963-2238
Key: Inn; 3 units; Moderate-Exp.; Limited smoking; No children under 13; No credit cards

This early 1900s Victorian home offers a big front porch with mountain views in a quiet residential neighborhood. Guest rooms are furnished with antiques and are decorated in pastel colors; a downstairs room features a separate entrance. The cozy living room offers a fireplace, and each evening wine with pâtes or cheeses is served. A gourmet breakfast is served at 9:00 A.M.; both breakfast and wine are offered on the large veranda, weather permitting.

The Cinnamon Bear

1407 Kearney Street, St. Helena, CA 94574
Phone: (707) 963-4653
Key: Inn; 4 units; Expensive; No smoking; No children under 11; Credit cards

This charming 1904 house sits in a quiet residential neighborhood. The homey atmosphere is created by comfortable antiques and, yes, lots of bears, mainly of the stuffed variety. All guest rooms have a bath of their own, and guests enjoy a large parlor and dining room. The "Relatives" suite on the main floor offers two rooms, a queen-size bed, a large claw-foot tub, and lots of privacy. Complimentary wine and hor d'oeuvres are served in the early evening; the full homemade breakfast varies each morning.

Cornerstone Bed & Breakfast Inn

1308 Main Street, St. Helena, CA 94574
Phone: (707) 963-1891
Key: Inn/Hotel; 12 units; Moderate; Smoking OK; No children under 11; Credit cards

Built originally as a hotel in 1891, this hotel b&b has been completely refurbished. The corner b&b, constructed of cut, local stone, is located in the heart of town within walking distance of shops, restaurants, and a few wineries. The dozen guest rooms, with washing facilities in each and baths across the hall, are fully air-conditioned and feature some of the original hotel furnishings. A continental breakfast is offered on the sideboard, and guests may eat in the privacy of their rooms or at the large dining table. A parlor with antiques in the site of afternoon wine.

Creekside Inn

945 Main Street, St. Helena, CA 94574
Phone: (707) 963-7244
Key: Inn; 3 units; Moderate; No smoking; No children; No credit cards

The pleasant murmurs of White Sulphur Creek and ancient oaks give a country setting to this inn located in the heart of the town. The individually decorated guest rooms feature an antique oak poster bed and white iron beds, all with a French country feel. Guests are served a full breakfast each morning in the sun room or creekside on the patio. Innkeepers will cater a candlelight dinner in the dining room upon arrangement.

Deer Run

3995 Spring Mountain Road, St. Helena, CA 94574
Phone: (707) 963-3794
Key: Home; 2 units; Moderate; No smoking; No children; No credit cards

This small b&b offers a secluded mountain retreat overlooking the valley vineyards. Both of the guest accommodations have a private bath; one features a fireplace. A pool is available, and a continental breakfast is served each morning offering fresh fruit, juice, bran or blueberry muffins, and fruit breads.

Elsie's Conn Valley Inn

726 Rossi Road, St. Helena, CA 94574
Phone: (707) 963-4614
Key: Home; 2 units; Moderate; No smoking; No children; No credit cards

Four miles outside of town is this country retreat with lawns and gardens as well as views of the vineyards and rolling hills. The home b&b with stone pillars in front offers two comfortable bedrooms to guests, each with a garden view and private bath. Upon arrival guests are given a basket of fruit, cheeses, and crackers to accompany a bottle of Napa Valley wine. The breakfast offering, served inside or on the patio, comprises homemade breads and pastries, fruits, juices, and beverages. Guests at Elsie's may relax by the fire, watch television in the guests' own family room, or stroll along country roads to nearby Lake Hennessey.

Erika's Hillside, St. Helena

Erika's Hillside

285 Fawn Park Road, St. Helena, CA 94574
Phone: (707) 963-2887
Key: Inn; 3 units; Moderate-Exp.; Limited smoking; Children on approval; No credit cards

The English Tudor inn on three acres of beautifully landscaped grounds enjoys views of the vineyards and wineries. The spacious guest accommodations include rooms and a suite, all with private entrances and views of the valley. The continental breakfast, served on the patio or deck or in the garden room, features German specialties. Guests are welcomed with a glass of local wine.

The Farmhouse

St. Helena, CA 94574
Phone: (707) 944-8430
Key: Home; 3 units; Moderate-Exp.; No smoking; No children under 13; No credit cards

This seventy-year-old Mission-style farmhouse is nestled amidst vineyards on a tree-lined country lane. The home, with ten bedrooms, offers three to guests: one large room with antiques, a queen-size bed, color TV, and bath, and two rooms in the "girls" wing that share one bath. Guests are invited to swim in the pool, sip wine in the courtyard, and enjoy the continental breakfast featuring fruits from the farm. The innkeepers at this home b&b discourage drop-in guests and prefer phone reservations only.

Harvest Inn

One Main Street, St. Helena, CA 94574
Phone: (707) 963-9463
Key: Inn/Hotel; 25 units; Moderate-Del.; Limited smoking; Children OK; Credit cards

This large Tudor-style inn was built in 1978 on the grounds of a twenty-one-acre working vineyard. Besides enjoying the grounds, guests may swim in the pool during the summer and relax in the spa year round. All guest rooms have king- or queen-size beds, color TV, telephone, and antique decor; and most also have fireplaces, wet bars, and refrigerators. A continental breakfast of pastry and rolls, fresh fruit, and juices is served.

Hotel St. Helena

1309 Main Street, St. Helena, CA 94574
Phone: (707) 963-4388
Key: Inn/Hotel; 18 units; Moderate-Exp.; Smoking OK; No children; Credit cards

The 1881 hotel on the town's Main Street was completely renovated and carefully restored a few years ago. Today, the hotel offers guest rooms upstairs decorated in antiques, authentic wallpapers, quilted spreads, armoires, and carpeting. The downstairs is devoted to shops and a comfortable sitting area, where the morning breakfast buffet, as well as evening sherry, is served.

The Ink House

1575 St. Helena Highway, St. Helena, CA 94574
Phone: (707) 963-3890
Key: Inn; 3 units; Moderate; No smoking; No children under 12; No credit cards

The historic 1884 home is Italianate Victorian and boasts twelve- and eleven-foot-high ceilings. The guest rooms, with private bath, have handmade quilts, lace curtains, and antiques. Guests may enjoy an antique-filled parlor that features a restored 1870 pump organ. A continental breakfast of juice and home-baked nut breads is served buffet style in the dining room.

Judy's Bed & Breakfast

2036 Madrona Avenue, St. Helena, CA 94574
Phone: (707) 963-3081
Key: Home; 1 unit; Moderate; No smoking; Children OK; No credit cards

Vineyards surround this ranch-style b&b on three sides. The one suite consists of a bedroom, sitting room, and private bath and entrance. The quarters are decorated in antiques with a

86

queen-size brass bed, air conditioning, and color TV. Freshly baked goodies are served in the room or by the pool, which is available to guests. The suite is supplied with wine, cheese, fruit, and candies.

Judy's Ranch House

701 Rossi Road, St. Helena, CA 94574
Phone: (707) 963-3081
Key: Home; 2 units; Moderate-Exp.; No smoking; Children OK; No credit cards

This spacious ranch-style b&b boasts a unique open-air courtyard in the center of the house, a large living room with fireplace, and magnificent views of the valley countryside. Guests may either sip wine and enjoy cheese, crackers, and fruit on the front porch overlooking the oaks and creek or unwind in the Jacuzzi spa with pasture views. Each of the guest accommodations, furnished in a combination of contemporary and antique decor, offers an oversized bed, ceiling fan, private bath, and hillside views. A complimentary continental breakfast of orange juice, fresh fruit, pastries, and coffee or tea is served in the sunny country kitchen.

Milat Vineyard

1091 St. Helena Highway So., St. Helena, CA 94574
Phone: (707) 963-2612
Key: Guest house; 2 units; Moderate; Smoking OK; No children; No credit cards

Surrounded by the family-operated vineyard, this guest cottage boasts both privacy and spectacular views. Guests enjoy continental breakfast each morning served in the guest house or on the private patio.

Oliver House

2970 Silverado Trail, St. Helena, CA 94574
Phone: (707) 963-4089
Key: Inn; 5 units; Expensive-Del.; No smoking; Children OK; No credit cards

This chalet-style b&b sits in the foothills overlooking vineyards. Each room is decorated in antiques and has a French door leading to balcony views of the countryside. An old-fashioned parlor adjoins the guest rooms and offers relaxation in front of the fireplace. The continental breakfast featuring berries or fruit fresh from the garden is served in the country kitchen or on the balcony.

Prager Winery B&B

1281 Lewelling Lane, St. Helena, CA 94574
Phone: (707) 963-3720
Key: Cottage; 1 unit; Expensive; Smoking OK; Children OK; No credit cards

This home b&b with separate guest accommodation is located right on the winery premises. The "Winery" suite is situated above the barrel-aging cellar and offers a private entrance, bath, bedroom, living room, and a veranda with views of the vineyard and mountains. The home-baked breakfast is served in the suite, and guests enjoy a personal tour of the winery.

Spanish Villa

474 Glass Mountain Road, St. Helena, CA 94574
Phone: (707) 963-7483
Key: Inn; 3 units; Moderate; No smoking; No children; No credit cards

The two-story Spanish-style villa is surrounded by country roads and woods. Its Mediterranean design features an enclosed patio, a Jacuzzi, and a spacious sitting room with arched windows. The guest rooms all have king-size beds, private baths, and handmade glass replicas of the famous Tiffany lamp. Of course, breakfast is included in the stay.

Sutter Home Inn

225 St. Helena Highway, St. Helena, CA 94574
Phone: (707) 963-4423
Key: Inn; 9 units; Moderate-Exp.; No smoking; No children; Credit cards

This inn, formerly the Chalet Bernensis, is located on the grounds adjoining the Sutter Home Winery. The chalet now houses the winery office and serves as the lobby for guests. The nine accommodations for guests are situated both in the "Water Tower," a replica of the original Victorian tower, which offers private baths, fireplaces, and air conditioning, and in the "Carriage House," a more recent addition. The rooms have been completely redecorated and are surrounded by peaceful Victorian gardens. Guests enjoy breakfast in the glassed-in sun porch of the old home.

Villa St. Helena

2727 Sulphur Springs Avenue, St. Helena, CA 94574
Phone: (707) 963-2514
Key: Inn; 4 units; Expensive-Del.; Limited smoking; No children; Credit cards

This 12,000-square-foot, three-level brick mansion on a secluded, wooded hillside offers panoramic views of Napa Valley and twenty acres filled with walking trails, a courtyard, and a swimming pool. The former (1940s and 1950s) celebrity hideaway gives its b&b guests a luxurious retreat. The beamed-ceilinged living room and its massive stone fireplace was used recently in TV's "Falcon Crest" filming. A generous, homemade continental breakfast is served in a solarium. The four guest rooms, with private baths and private entrance verandas, have a country ele-

Villa St. Helena, St. Helena

gance accomplished by the use of antiques and muted, earth-tone color schemes. Some of the rooms feature fireplaces. Guests also are treated to the inn's private label wine.

The White Ranch

707 White Lane, St. Helena, CA 94574
Phone: (707) 963-4635
Key: Home; 1 unit; Moderate; No smoking; No children; No credit cards

This farmhouse, built in 1865, offers sherry on the front porch and a picnic table for lunch or supper. The guest suite, decorated in antiques, has a bedroom, dressing room, and private bath. Guests may enjoy the fireplace in the parlor. The morning continental breakfast consists of juice, homemade breads and jams, and espresso coffee.

Wine Country Cottage

P.O. Box 295, 400 Meadowood Lane, St. Helena, CA 94574
Phone: (707) 963-4633
Key: Cottage; 1 unit; Moderate; Smoking OK; Children OK; No credit cards

This charming cottage nestled among the elms and pines provides guests with privacy and quiet. The single cottage contains a bedroom/living room, complete kitchen, bath, and patio. Guests choose between a complimentary continental breakfast, in bed or on the patio, or a champagne feast for an additional charge. Innkeepers will also arrange for mud baths or massages, hot-air ballooning, and dinner.

The Wine Country Inn, St. Helena

The Wine Country Inn

1152 Lodi Lane, St. Helena, CA 94574
Phone: (707) 963-7077
Key: Inn/Hotel; 25 units; Expensive; Smoking OK; No children under 12; Credit cards

The small country hotel is located off a busy highway in a peaceful setting. Most of the guest accommodations boast rural views, and some have patios, balconies, or fireplaces usable fall through spring. All rooms have private bath and are decorated uniquely in country antiques and fresh colors. A buffet-style continental breakfast is served each morning. A beautiful pool and spa have recently been added for guests' enjoyment.

Gee-Gee's B&B

7810 Sonoma Highway, Santa Rosa, CA 95405
Phone: (707) 833-6667
Key: Home/Cottage; 4 units; Moderate; No smoking; No children; No credit cards

This converted farmhouse and cottage situated on a full acre offers guests a swimming pool, decks, and a sitting room with TV and fireplace. Two of the guest accommodations are located in the main house and share one bath, and the other two are housed in the separate cottage. A tasty, full breakfast is served on the deck overlooking orchards, vineyards, and mountains. Bicycles are complimentary.

Melitta Station Inn

5850 Melita Road, Santa Rosa, CA 95409
Phone: (707) 538-7712
Key: Inn; 6 units; Moderate; Limited smoking; Children on approval; Credit cards

In the late 1880s the long redwood barn structure was a stagecoach stop, then went on to be a freight station, general store, boarding house, and antique shop. Carefully converted to a b&b inn and home, the interiors reflect a country feel with antiques and hand stencilings. The comfortably furnished guest rooms have private baths. A sitting room features a wood-burning stove, a sideboard with wine, and French door views of the countryside. The breakfast of homemade scones, cheese tarts, and fruit is served on the deck. Guests enjoy the inn's beautiful setting, which is surrounded by parks offering hiking and other forms of recreation.

Pygmalion House

331 Orange Street, Santa Rosa, CA 95401
Phone: (707) 526-3407
Key: Inn; 5 units; Inexpensive-Mod.; No smoking; No children under 10; Credit cards

This historic Victorian home with twelve-foot-high ceilings is near downtown Santa Rosa. The five guest rooms all have private baths with old-fashioned claw-foot tubs or showers and an eclectic country decor. Guests enjoy a parlor with fireplace and TV and evening wine, cheese, and nuts. The full breakfast served in the country kitchen includes such delicacies as cereals, muffins, croissants, ham, egg dishes, and the inn's own blend of brewed decaf coffee.

Vintners Inn

4350 Barnes Road, Santa Rosa, CA 95401
Phone: (707) 575-7350; (800) 421-2584
Key: Inn/Hotel; 44 units; Moderate-Del.; Limited smoking; Children OK; Credit cards

A small French "village," with a central plaza and fountain surrounded by four separate stucco and red tile-roof buildings with arched windows, has been created in the middle of a working vineyard as a unique b&b offering. The hotel offers forty-four individually decorated, spacious guest rooms furnished in a country French motif with antique pine furniture; some have wood-burning fireplaces, custom-made pine beds, beamed ceilings, color TV, telephones, private baths, and balcony or patio views of the plaza or vineyards. A common building contains a library and breakfast area, where juices and hot breads are served each morning. The inn may accommodate executive conferences, with separate conference and dining rooms also available. Recent additions to the inn include a large sun deck with spa and the John Ash & Co. restaurant, specializing in Sonoma regional cuisine.

East Wing of the Merry M Ranch

P.O. Box 17, Rutherford, CA 94573
Phone: (707) 963-3379
Key: Inn; 1 unit; Expensive; Smoking OK; Children OK; Credit cards

This second-story suite is reached by a private circular staircase and consists of a sitting room, bedroom, shower/bath, and full deck that overlooks the vineyards. Comfortable antiques and oriental rugs decorate throughout, and extras such as in-room coffee and tea, ice, and wine glasses are available. The complimentary full breakfast is served at the nearby Rancho Caymus Inn.

Rancho Caymus Inn

P.O. Box 78, 1140 Rutherford Road, Rutherford, CA 94573
Phone: (707) 963-1777
Key: Inn/Hotel; 26 units; Expensive-Del.; Smoking OK; No children under 5; Credit cards

This unique stucco inn with red tile roof encircles a small, quiet central garden. The twenty-six guest rooms contain two levels featuring sitting rooms with polished oak floors, wool rugs, comfortable seating, and (in the twenty rooms on the first floor) hand-sculpted adobe fireplaces. Guests step up to the bedroom with black-walnut queen-size beds, other handworked furnishings, and French doors that open onto a private garden patio or balcony. All rooms feature hand-hewn beams, eighty-year-old handmade doors, air conditioning, color TV, telephones, and luxurious bathrooms with stoneware basins and hardwood countertops. Four "Getaway" master suites offer full kitchens, stained-glass windows, and Jacuzzi tubs. The Caymus Kitchen restaurant, open for breakfast and lunch, serves a "Hacienda" continental breakfast in the room or in the award-winning garden.

Bordeaux House

P.O. Box 2766, Yountville, CA 94599
Phone: (707) 944-2855
Key: Inn/Cottage; 6 units; Expensive-Del.; Smoking OK; Children OK (cottages only); No credit cards

The formal red-brick structure situated among lush gardens and large pines is secluded from the main highway yet convenient to the famous wineries in the area. The spacious rooms in hues of camel and wine reds are air-conditioned and also boast fireplaces, private baths, and patios for the evening glass of wine. A continental breakfast is served each morning.

Burgundy House

P.O. Box 2766, Yountville, CA 94599
Phone: (707) 944-2855
Key: Inn/Cottage; 9 units; Moderate; Smoking OK; Children OK
(cottages only); No credit cards

Built in the 1870s of native stone from the surrounding countryside, this inn once served as a brandy distillery and bread bakery. The breakfast is served in the downstairs hearth room, also the locale of late-afternoon wine sampling. Guest rooms, appointed with antiques, overlook fields of grapes.

Magnolia Hotel

P.O. Drawer M, 6529 Yount Street, Yountville, CA 94599
Phone: (707) 944-2056
Key: Inn/Hotel/Cottage; 12 units; Moderate-Del.; No smoking; No
children; No credit cards

This 1873 hotel features a large swimming pool and Jacuzzi spa on the grounds. The guest rooms, all with private bath, are furnished in antiques. Some rooms boast balconies, fireplaces, patios, extra-high ceilings, or bay windows; accommodations are available in the main hotel or in the garden court. A full breakfast is served promptly at 9:00 A.M. each morning; a crystal decanter of port wine is available in each guest room. A carriage-house suite has recently been added.

Napa Valley Railway Inn

P.O. Box 2568, 6503 Washington Street, Yountville, CA 94599
Phone: (707) 944-2000
Key: Inn; 9 units; Moderate-Exp.; Smoking OK; Children OK;
Credit cards

Nine brightly painted, turn-of-the-century railroad cars from several different railway lines sit alongside the original Napa Valley Railroad tracks and have been renovated to form this unique inn. The three cabooses and six railcars overlooking vineyards offer nine guest room suites, all with private baths, queen-size beds, and sitting rooms with velvet love seats. Many rooms feature skylights and bay windows. This cozy bed and "hospitality" inn serves wine in the afternoon, and in-room coffee and tea are available at all times. Breakfast may be enjoyed at one of several restaurants in the adjacent Vintage 1870 complex of shops but is not included in the stay.

Oleander House

7433 St. Helena Highway, P.O. Box 2937, Yountville, CA 94599
Phone: (707) 944-8315
Key: Inn; 4 units; Moderate; No smoking; No children; Credit cards

This spacious, two-story home located at the entrance to Napa Valley offers four guest rooms. Each accommodation features high ceilings, queen-size brass bed, antiques, private bath, balcony, and fireplace. Guests enjoy complimentary wine and sherry, and an ample breakfast is served around the large pine table in the dining room.

The Webber Place

P.O. Box 2873, Yountville, CA 94599
Phone: (707) 944-8384
Key: Inn; 4 units; Moderate-Exp.; Limited smoking; No children under 12; Credit cards

This converted farmhouse, within walking distance of town shops, features guest rooms furnished in antiques, two with in-room claw-foot tubs. The "Veranda Suite" has a private, latticed veranda and unusual woodwork. Included is a breakfast of fresh fruit, homemade muffins, juice, and coffee, as well as wine in the afternoon.

Beltane Ranch

P.O. Box 395, 11775 Sonoma Highway, Glen Ellen, CA 95442
Phone: (707) 996-6501
Key: Inn; 3 units; Moderate; Smoking OK; No children under 8;
No credit cards

This 1892 house is situated on a mountain slope with sweeping views of the Sonoma Valley vineyards. The active ranch raises both grapes and sheep, and its comfortable guest accommodations all boast private baths and entrances. A generous breakfast, along with views, is served on the porch on warmer days.

Glenelly Inn

5131 Warm Springs Road, Glen Ellen, CA 95442
Phone: (707) 996-6720
Key: Inn; 6 units; Moderate; No smoking; No children under 15;
Credit cards

This b&b was built in 1916 as an inn and was a popular summer retreat for city dwellers in the 1920s. The inn, restored carefully to its original glory, offers to guests once again its long verandas with wicker furniture, an acre of shady lawn, and "Common Room" with cobblestone fireplace and French leaded-glass windows. The six individually decorated guest rooms all boast private baths and entrances as well as iron, brass, or four-poster beds (except one trundle unit), some Laura Ashley linens, and pleasantly coordinated prints. The "Coleraine" room features a unique queen-size, pewter-and-brass bed. Each afternoon guests may sample local wine and cheeses, and the generous continental breakfast is offered each morning on the veranda under a large oak tree or by fireside in the "Common Room" on chilly days.

Au Relais Bed & Breakfast Inn

691 Broadway, Sonoma, CA 95476
Phone: (707) 996-1031

97

Au Relais Bed & Breakfast Inn, Sonoma

Key: Inn; 4 units; Moderate; No smoking; Children OK; Credit cards

This late-1800s Victorian residence with an award-winning restaurant of the same name next door is within walking distance of Sonoma Plaza and boasts beautifully landscaped yards. The guest rooms at the inn, in shades of rose, offer fresh flowers, fine antiques, quilts, ceiling fans, iron and brass beds, and both private and shared baths. Guests enjoy an outdoor cabana and a cozy parlor with glowing fireplace. Drinks and hor d'oeuvres are available from the restaurant upon request. A generous continental breakfast is served in the inn's own dining room each morning.

Chalet Bed & Breakfast

18935 Fifth Street West, Sonoma, CA 95476
Phone: (707) 996-0190/938-3129
Key: Inn/Cottage; 5 units; Moderate-Exp.; Smoking OK; Children OK in cottage (OK in house mid-week only); No credit cards

This farmhouse with cottage is situated on three acres where fruit, nuts, and eggs are produced, just three-quarters of a mile from the town of Sonoma. In the main house, two upstairs rooms share a sitting room and bath, as do the two downstairs rooms. The private cottage with bath, wood-burning stove, and kitchen facilities has a loft. A full country breakfast is included, as is use of the hot tub.

El Dorado Inn, Sonoma

El Dorado Inn

405 First Street West, Sonoma, CA 95476
Phone: (707) 996-3030
Key: Inn/Hotel/Cottage; 30 units; Moderate-Exp.; Smoking OK; Children OK; Credit cards

This hotel b&b has been elegantly reconstructed from one of Sonoma's first adobe structures, built by Vallejo in 1837. The two-story, Monterey colonial home is now an L-shaped inn with the same redwood planking and paned windows curving around a beautifully landscaped courtyard, which has one of the state's oldest fig trees. The interior of the inn features muted shades of burgundy, antiques, leaded glass, brass, and a magnificent oak staircase. Guests may enjoy the saloon, a large lounge with fireplace, and a country French dining room. The guest rooms and suites, offering both private and shared baths, have king-, queen-, or twin-size beds and views of the hills, plaza, or courtyard. Garden cottages offer private baths. A complimentary breakfast is served beside the stone fireplace in the lounge.

Sonoma Hotel

110 West Spain Street, Sonoma, CA 95476
Phone: (707) 996-2996
Key: Inn/Hotel; 17 units; Moderate-Exp.; Smoking OK; Children OK; Credit cards

The exact age of the old hotel is unknown, but records show it to be at least of 1870s vintage. The hotel has been completely restored; the guest accommodations have been furnished with authentic items from the days of the Barbary Coast and the Gay Nineties. Interesting antiques include a bedroom suite owned by General Vallejo's sister and the original chandeliers. A restaurant is a recent addition to the establishment and offers dinners and brunches, with menus changing weekly.

Thistle Dew Inn

P.O. Box 1326, 171 West Spain Street, Sonoma, CA 95476
Phone: (707) 938-2909
Key: Inn; 6 units; Inexpensive-Mod.; Limited smoking; No children; Credit cards

The inn is located in a quiet residential neighborhood just three doors off the main plaza. It consists of two one-story Victorian houses surrounded by lawns and gardens and decorated in collector's pieces of Mission style. The guest rooms, some with private bath, have washstands, ceilings fans, and air conditioning. A full breakfast is served in the dining room, and appetizers and wine are offered on the deck each evening, weather permitting. Bicycles and picnic baskets are available for guests' use.

Trojan Horse Inn

P.O. Box 1663, 19455 Sonoma Highway, Sonoma, CA 95476
Phone: (707) 996-2430
Key: Inn; 8 units; Moderate; No smoking; No children; Credit cards

This 1887 Victorian, farm-style home sits on the banks of Sonoma Creek. The inn, painted three shades of blue, has been completely renovated. Outside features two levels of well-kept gardens and patios, beautiful old trees, and a spa. The inn is furnished in English and French antiques, and most guest rooms offer queen-size beds, plush linens and bedspreads, ceiling fans, and air conditioning. The five shared-bath accommodations have in-room vanities. The innkeeper is a porcelain-doll maker, and her collection, which is also for sale, decorates the rooms of the inn. A full breakfast with home-baked goodies and a hot dish is served graciously in the dining room each morning; wine and cheese are offered in the early evening.

Victorian Garden Inn, Sonoma

Victorian Garden Inn

316 E. Napa Street, Sonoma, CA 95476
Phone: (707) 996-5339
Key: Inn; 4 units; Moderate-Exp.; Limited smoking; No children; Credit cards

This 1800s farmhouse with watchtower features a secluded acre with meandering walks through creekside Victorian gardens. Guest rooms are individually furnished in antiques with quaint wallcoverings, and all but one have private baths. One guest accommodation has a fireplace, private entrance, and claw-foot tub. A generous continental breakfast may be enjoyed in the dining room or carried on a wicker tray to the room. During the day guests may swim in the garden-set pool, walk to shops, or relax on the creekside patio.

Arbor Guest House, Napa

Arbor Guest House

1436 G Street, Napa, CA 94559
Phone: (707) 252-8144
Key: Inn; 4 units; Moderate-Exp.; No smoking; No children under 11; Credit cards

Trumpet vines and hanging fuchsia cover the arbor that connects this award-winning Victorian home and carriage house. A garden motif is featured inside the inn with wallcoverings, period antiques, and beveled glass. Guest rooms in the main house and in the carriage house are beautifully appointed with antiques, private baths, and queen-size beds. "Rose's Bower" features a romantic fireplace faced by rose-patterned French chairs. Guests are served a generous breakfast of fresh fruits, cereals, and baked goods in the room, in the dining room, or on the patio surrounded by fruit and cedar trees.

Beazley House

1910 First Street, Napa, CA 94559
Phone: (707) 257-1649
Key: Inn/Cottage; 9 units; Moderate-Exp.; Limited smoking; No children under 13; Credit cards

Beazley House, Napa

This mansion with converted carriage house sits on one-half acre of landscaped grounds. Its turn-of-the-century character is expressed throughout in stained glass, inlaid floors, and antique-furnished rooms. Some of the guest rooms feature fireplaces, and the carriage-house accommodations have private spas and baths. The spacious living room is equipped with a teacart full of beverages. A generous continental breakfast is served in the dining room each morning.

The Chateau Hotel

4195 Solano Avenue, Napa, CA 94558
Phone: (707) 253-9300; (800) 253-NAPA
Key: Inn/Hotel; 115 units; Moderate-Del.; Smoking OK; Children OK; Credit cards

This recently opened hotel b&b resembles a European country inn. A hospitality room off the hotel lobby is a relaxing center for guests who enjoy reading and games and is the site of a generous complimentary breakfast each morning and a wine-tasting social each evening. Other extras include daily newspapers, in-room movies, a heated swimming pool, and Jacuzzi. The one hundred and fifteen guest rooms have custom decor featuring provincial wallcoverings, country fabrics, and traditional furnishings and boast ceramic-tile baths and color TV. As a unique bonus, you may reserve a ride in this b&b's very own hot-air balloon.

Coombs Residence Inn on the Park

720 Seminary Street, Napa, CA 94559
Phone: (707) 257-0789
Key: Inn; 4 units; Moderate-Exp.; Limited smoking; No children under 12; Credit cards

This gracious 1852 Victorian home faces the park and is framed by trees, year-round blooms, and lawn. Guests enjoy a swimming pool, Jacuzzi, and bicycles for riding around the park. The inn has been completely restored and furnished with American and European antiques. All guest rooms except one share baths and offer down quilts and pillows, lace sheets, and terry robes. The breakfast of freshly ground coffee, fresh fruit, fruit breads or muffins, and croissants is served in the living room or on the pool-side deck; the morning fare is presented on fine china with silver and linens. Guests enjoy wine, cheese, and fruit in the evening; sherry and port are available in a formal parlor complete with fireplace and stereo. Guests may help themselves to sodas in the kitchen any time at this hospitable b&b.

Country Garden Inn

1815 Silverado Trail, Napa, CA 94558
Phone: (707) 255-1197
Key: Inn; 7 units; Moderate-Del.; No smoking; No children under 16; Credit cards

This nineteenth-century coach house on the Silverado Trail is a true English-style country inn on one and one-half acres of mature woodland and riverside property with rose gardens, fountains, lawns, and abundant maple trees. The b&b is furnished throughout in English pine antiques and family heirlooms; the romantic oak-beamed public rooms boast pastel colors, a carved fruitwood fireplace, and French doors that open onto a deck and terrace overlooking the river. The spacious and elegant guest rooms feature private baths (two with Jacuzzis), air conditioning, oversized beds, and color-coordinated linens; three rooms boast private river-view decks. A separate cottage with wood-burning fireplace is available. The "Morning Room" is the site of a full champagne breakfast that includes a fruit buffet, homemade scones and coffee cake, and hot entree such as eggs Benedict. Guests at this hospitable inn also are treated to in-room wine, afternoon tea, late-evening desserts, and a happy hour before dinner with hors d'oeuvres.

Gallery Osgood, Napa

Gallery Osgood

2230 First Street, Napa, CA 94559
Phone: (707) 224-0100
Key: Inn; 3 units; Moderate; Smoking OK; No children under 13; Credit cards

This gracious residence surrounded by extensive flower gardens and trees was built in 1898. Today, the Queen Anne hosts both a small b&b and a fine art-and-craft gallery. The three guest rooms with air conditioning, which share an Art Deco bath, are decorated in specially selected antiques, prints, and tapestries. Complimentary wine is served in the sitting room, and a lavish breakfast is presented with fine china, crystal, and silver each morning. The full breakfast includes such delicacies as open-face omelettes, crêpes and wild rice, and mushroom pancakes. Guests sip wine or morning coffee on the gazebo.

The Goodman House

1225 Division Street, Napa, CA 94558
Phone: (707) 257-1166
Key: Inn; 4 units; Moderate; No smoking; Children on approval; Credit cards

This late-1870s house combines both old and new to create a comfortable b&b. The spacious guest rooms share a bath (except for the master suite), and each has its own special charm. The dining room is the site of morning croissants and melon, while the upstairs kitchen is available to guests for a cup of coffee, a snack, glass of wine, and sight-seeing hints. The "Red Room" offers relaxation with a grand piano and fireplace.

La Belle Epoque

1386 Calistoga Avenue, Napa, CA 94559
Phone: (707) 257-2161
Key: Inn; 4 units; Moderate-Exp.; Limited smoking; No children; No credit cards

This Queen Anne-Victorian home boasts impressive stained-glass windows and is decorated throughout in period antiques and original art. Guest accommodations include two rooms with private bath and two with semi-private baths that share a shower. Guests at the inn are invited to taste premium vintage wines in the wine cellar and are served a generous continental breakfast in the sunny garden room.

La Residence Country Inn

4066 St. Helena Highway, Napa, CA 94558
Phone: (707) 253-0337
Key: Inn; 20 units; Moderate-Del.; Smoking OK; No children; Credit cards

This 1870 Gothic Revival home called the "Mansion" and a French country barn called the "Cabernet Hall" offer guest rooms and suites with private baths, fireplaces, and French and English pine and American oak antiques. Modern amenities include central air conditioning, a swimming pool, and a spa. Guests at La Residence enjoy evening wine and breakfast served by the innkeepers.

Napa Inn, Napa

Napa Inn

1137 Warren Street, Napa, CA 94558
Phone: (707) 257-1444
Key: Inn; 4 units; Moderate; Smoking OK; Children OK; No credit cards

This turn-of-the-century home is in a tree-lined residential section of town yet convenient to the local winery, shopping, and ballooning activities. The spacious rooms are actually suites, and all but one have refrigerators. A continental breakfast is served in the room each morning. A unique dining area with restored church pews has been created in one room.

The Old World Inn, Napa

The Old World Inn

1301 Jefferson Street, Napa, CA 94559
Phone: (707) 257-0112
Key: Inn; 8 units; Moderate-Exp.; No smoking; No children; Credit cards

This 1906 home with shady porches and beveled glass contains interior decor inspired by Swedish artist Carl Larrson. A fireside parlor has bright Scandinavian colors and offers soft classical music. The guest rooms, in French blues, pinks, peaches, and greens, feature Victorian and antique furniture, private baths with mostly claw-foot tubs, canopy beds, and skylights. Special guest amenities include a custom Jacuzzi, evening wine in the room, and international cheeses and a selection of homemade goodies before retiring. The generous breakfast is served in the "Morning Room" with old-fashioned English hospitality.

Sybron House

7400 St. Helena Highway, Napa, CA 94558
Phone: (707) 944-2785
Key: Inn; 3 units; Expensive; No smoking; No children under 13; No credit cards

This new Victorian-style home, built in 1978, is situated on a hill overlooking the valley. Guests may enjoy the whole house, including the wet bar stocked with wine, cheese, crackers, coffee, tea, and hot chocolate. The continental breakfast features croissants and nut breads as well as juice and fresh fruit. A tennis court and spa are also available to guests at the inn.

The Village Inn

1012 Darms Lane, Napa, CA 94558
Phone: (707) 257-2089
Key: Cottages; 8 units; Moderate-Exp.; Smoking OK; Children OK; No credit cards

This country retreat on two wooded acres is composed of eight separate cottages, all individually decorated. Each features a living room with sofa bed, bedroom with queen-size bed, bathroom, kitchen, and air conditioning and heating. The continental breakfast arrives in a basket when the guest desires, and complimentary wine is offered each evening.

Freitas House Inn

744 Jackson Street, Fairfield, CA 94533
Phone: (707) 425-1366; (800) 782-1800 (CA only)
Key: Inn; 6 units; Moderate-Exp.; Limited smoking; No children under 12; Credit cards

This 1925 English Tudor mansion on a historic downtown corner is surrounded by old cloistered gardens and stately trees. The interior has a large, open, mahogany staircase and mahogany woodwork, large brass chandeliers, and antiques. Guest rooms include antique- and rattan-furnished accommodations in the main house and two deluxe suites in a separate carriage house. Upon arrival, guests are treated to wine and freshly baked pretzels with mustard. Breakfast, beginning with a tray outside the door carrying juice, coffee, and the newspaper, is followed by a hearty buffet downstairs featuring quiche, crêpes, and a homemade nut ring. Guests enjoy the antique-filled living room, an adjacent sunroom with TV, and a backyard swing and Ping-Pong.

CALIFORNIA GOLD COUNTRY

To Clio & Quincy Soda Springs *To Reno*
Nevada City Truckee
20 80 Olympic 89 Kings Beach
Grass Valley Valley
Yuba City Colfax Tahoe City *Lake Tahoe*
49 Georgetown *NEVADA*
Newcastle Auburn
Coloma
Davis 99 Placerville 50 Hope Valley
SACRAMENTO 49
80 88 395
Amador City Volcano
Sutter Creek 4
Ione Jackson 108
To 99 Murphys 395
San Francisco San Andreas *Mono Lake*
Columbia
STOCKTON Sonora Twain Harte
Jamestown Soulsbyville
Tuolumne 120

LEGEND: *Yosemite*
━━━ Freeway Route *Modesto* 49 *National* 395
──── Highway Route *Park*
○ Listed City or Town Mariposa
○ *Location Reference* 99 *To Bishop*
◎ LARGER CITY 140 To Mammoth
Merced Lakes
41

NORTH 99 *Madera* *Kings Canyon*
Scale in Miles *National Park*
0 10 20 30 40 50 *FRESNO*
CALIFORNIA GOLD COUNTRY 180
To Taft & Orosi

Communities born of the gold-rush days, old mines, vineyards, rolling hills with oaks, lakes, museums, the Sierras' grandeur, unlimited recreation, and the cornucopian fields of the great Central Valley make up this region's diverse character. The traveler may still pan gold here or tour the state's preserved gold-rush town, Columbia, or a thriving historic town, such as Sutter Creek, Amador, Jackson, or Nevada City—all steeped in the history of the "golden days." Nestled high in the Sierra Nevada are the communities of Tahoe City, Kings Beach, and Olympic Valley, which, still rich in history, are better known for their nearby casinos, skiing, and lake sports and beaches. The state's capital, Sacramento, offers history in the making as well as its Old Town to explore. History, the lure of gold-rush days, recreation, and scenic paradise—Gold Country's generous offerings are waiting.

The Feather Bed, Quincy

The Feather Bed

P.O. Box 3200, 542 Jackson Street, Quincy, CA 95971
Phone: (916) 283-0102
Key: Inn/Cottage; 6 units; Moderate; No smoking; No children under 15; Credit cards

111

Situated near downtown Quincy and surrounded by the trees and meadows of a national forest is this 1893 Queen Anne home with 1905 Greek Revival touches. The b&b with a cozy cottage "honeymoon suite" has a large turn-of-the-century parlor with wood columns and a formal dining room, where winter breakfast is served. The antique-filled guest rooms all have private baths with brass fixtures and claw-foot tubs as well as showers. The unique accommodations range from "Edward's Room," with antique windows and fireplace, to the corner "Morning Room," with private balcony. A generous continental breakfast featuring baked pears and apples is served on the flower-filled patio in the spring and summer and in the room year-round. The inn offers a cross-country skiing package as well as fishing poles, bicycle, and day packs for guests' use.

White Sulphur Springs Ranch, Clio

White Sulphur Springs Ranch

P.O. Box 136, Clio, CA 96106
Phone: (916) 836-2387
Key: Inn/Cottage; 7 units; Moderate-Del.; No smoking; No children under 13; Credit cards

First established as a stagecoach stop in 1852 and later as a family-run ranch and hotel, the b&b is open to guests once again

after the complete restoration of the ho~ ~ings.
The ranch, on forty acres of hillside tir~ ~he
old ranch buildings, such as a black~ ~
sulphur-spring-fed, olympic-size r~ ~
contains many of the original ¹~ ~
tures a pump organ and a pian~ ~
guest rooms are uniquely ᵈ~ ~
turn-of-the-century wallc~ ~
Valley. New accommoᵈ~ ~
inal building that nᶜ~ ~ ath,
living room, and ᵈ~ ~st and
early morning c~ ~ nuts in
the parlor each eᵥ~ ~underway
at this "living" muₛ~ ~ıque b&b ride
that features a threε~ ~npagne break,
swim, and barbecue.

Bullard House

256 E. 1st Avenue, Chico, CA 95926
Phone: (916) 342-5912
Key: Home; 4 units; Moderate; No smoking; No children; No
credit cards

This 1902 home has been restored throughout, with care
taken to modernize only the essentials, such as plumbing and
electricity. The guest rooms are each unique and share two baths.
Guests have the freedom to enjoy the living room, parlor, and
dining room. A generous continental breakfast with homemade
muffins and breads is served each morning. Bikes are available for
touring the town or going to the local park for swimming, golfing,
or picnicking. Advance reservations are necessary.

Grandmere's Inn

449 Broad Street, Nevada City, CA 95959
Phone: (916) 265-4660
Key: Inn; 6 units; Moderate-Exp.; No smoking; Children OK (1
room only); Credit cards

This three-story Colonial Revival home with a two-story carriage house is listed in the National Register of Historic Places as the "Sargent House." The 7,300-square-foot home is surrounded by rolling lawns and Victorian gardens that present an ideal area for weddings and parties, for which a commercial kitchen and staff are available. The elegant guest rooms at the inn feature private baths and queen-size beds, and three have double sofa/sleepers as well. The inn is furnished in a country French motif with lots of antique pine, baskets, and American art. Guests enjoy a living room and dining room, where the full breakfast is served at 9:00 A.M.

Piety Hill Inn

523 Sacramento Street, Nevada City, CA 95959
Phone: (916) 265-2245
Key: Inn/Cottages; 7 units; Inexpensive; Smoking OK; No children; Credit cards

Originally built as an autocourt in the 1930s, this renovated enclave of guest cottages sits in a quiet residential neighborhood. The individual cottages surround a tree-shaded garden and lawn and are decorated, in an eclectic blend of the antique and the contemporary, with brass beds, hand stenciling, antique quilts, original art, and homey touches. Cottages also possess modern touches such as private baths, king-size beds, cable TV, and refrigerators. The breakfast is brought to the cottage and consists of a basket of pastries, fruit, juice, and beverages. A gazebo-crowned hot tub is nestled under a towering cedar at the edge of the garden.

Red Castle Inn

109 Prospect Street, Nevada City, CA 95959
Phone: (916) 265-5135
Key: Inn; 8 units; Inexpensive-Exp.; Limited smoking; Children on arrangement; No credit cards

Atop a hill overlooking picturesque Nevada City sits this four-story Gothic Revival structure resembling a castle. The im-

pressive, 1859-built brick mansion is a well-photographed historical landmark and has been an inn since 1963. It offers lush,
terraced gardens, verandas, and interiors filled with period antiques. The uniquely furnished guest rooms offer some historical
treasures, fresh flowers, and sweets; all but two rooms have private baths. The bountiful buffet breakfast, featuring family rec-
ipes, and afternoon high tea and sherry are both served in the
elegant parlor, where guests may play the 1880s pump organ.

National Hotel

211 Broad Street, Nevada City, CA 95959
Phone: (916) 265-4551
Key: Inn/Hotel; 43 units; Inexpensive-Mod.; Smoking OK; Chil-
dren OK; Credit cards

Claiming to be the "oldest continuously operating hotel west
of the Rocky Mountains," this registered historical landmark offers both hospitality and old-fashioned comfort. The hotel with
its distinctive cupola boasts a swimming pool filled with mountain water and a lobby with a square grand piano that journeyed
around Cape Horn. Most guest rooms and suites have a private
bath (thirteen rooms share baths) and are decorated in antiques
from the Gold Rush days that include some canopy beds. The
hotel has a complete Victorian restaurant and bar with banquet,
reception, and meeting facilities available; during summer, lunch
and dinner are served on the two-story veranda. Complimentary
coffee only is offered each morning at this bed and "hospitality"
inn.

The Mountain View Inn

P.O. Box 2011, Spring & High Streets, Truckee, CA 95734
Phone: (916) 587-5388
Key: Inn; 7 units; Inexpensive-Mod.; No smoking; Children OK;
Credit cards

This large Victorian home built in the 1880s has been completely restored and is highlighted by a hand-carved picket fence,

rich pine woodwork and unusual leather wainscoting in the hall. Five guest rooms share a bath upstairs and are decorated in soft tones and handmade Amish quilts; two rooms downstairs share a bath and can be a family suite. The dining room is the site of the full breakfast featuring omelettes, waffles, eggs Benedict, quiche, or French toast. The parlor serves as the locale for evening wine and cheese.

Truckee Hotel

P.O. Box 884, Truckee, CA 95734
Phone: (916) 587-4444
Key: Inn/Hotel; 40 units; Inexpensive-Mod.; Smoking OK; Children OK; Credit cards

This 1863 hotel nestled high in the Sierras is just a minute's walk from Amtrak and a few steps from the town's historic commercial center. The guest rooms, with private and shared baths, are a step into nineteenth-century California with sepia-toned portraits, oak antiques, canopies, and lace curtains. The bottom floor of the hotel features a fine restaurant and a saloon, and hotel guests receive a complimentary breakfast. Free guided tours of the hotel take place everyday, and champagne is added for special occasions.

Lake Tahoe Bed & Breakfast Inn

P.O. Box 177, 770 North Shore Blvd., Kings Beach, CA 95719
Phone: (916) 546-4441
Key: Home; 3 units; Moderate; Limited smoking; No children; No credit cards

The lake-view inn on the north side of Lake Tahoe is only two blocks from the beach and close to ski areas, casinos, and a public golf course. The large guest rooms have either queen- or king-size beds. A television and wood-burning fireplace are available to guests in the living room. A full continental breakfast is served. The inn is open from May 15 through October 1 only.

Cedar Tree Guest House

P.O. Box 7106, 612 Olympic Drive, Tahoe City, CA 95730
Phone: (916) 583-5421
Key: Home; 3 units; Inexpensive; No smoking; Children OK; No credit cards

This contemporary, wood-shingled house near the lake, a sandy beach, and pier offers three comfortable guest rooms, one with private bath. Guests may relax on large decks in the front, in the hot tub on the back deck, or in the loft with TV and VCR. Homemade rolls and muffins, fresh fruit, and coffee or tea are served in the dining area each morning. Bicycles and a barbecue are available at this guest house close to town. The b&b is open April through December only.

The Cottage Inn

P.O. Box 66, 1690 West Lake Boulevard, Tahoe City, CA 95730
Phone: (916) 581-4073
Key: Inn/Cottages; 14 units; Moderate-Exp.; No smoking; No children under 12; Credit cards

Five knotty-pine-paneled cottages on two acres of pine trees provide fourteen lodging accommodations at this b&b on the west shore of Lake Tahoe. The cottages cluster around a central garden area and boast private baths, European pine furniture, Scandinavian color schemes, cozy Pendleton blankets, and adjustable heating. Guests may choose either suites with living rooms or studios or the "Honeymoon" room with wood-burning fireplace. The main-house sitting room with its stone fireplace and piano is for guests' enjoyment, and breakfast is offered in the house dining room or in the cottage. The generous morning fare includes juice, fruit, granola, a cooked entree, and bread or muffins. Wine is offered on summer afternoon, hot cider or mulled wine in the winter. Some weekend dinners are available; guests may pay a nominal charge for evening espresso and homemade desserts.

Mayfield House

236 Grove Street, P.O. Box 2246, Tahoe City, CA 95730
Phone: (916) 583-1001
Key: Inn; 6 units; Moderate; Smoking OK; No children under 11;
Credit cards

This wood-and-stone inn with pretty gardens and patios offers a living room with cozy fireplace and individually decorated guest rooms. The six guest accommodations share three centrally located baths. Beds are covered with down comforters and pillows and fine linens. Breakfast, served in the room, on the patio, or in the breakfast area, includes such delectables as Finnish pancakes, Portuguese toast, apple strudel, and sweet-potato muffins. The menu changes daily, and all meals are served on fine china with fresh flowers.

Rockwood Lodge

P.O. Box 226, 5295 West Lake Boulevard, Homewood CA 95718
Phone: (916) 525-4663
Key: Inn; 4 units; Expensive-Del.; No smoking; No children; No credit cards

Hand-hewn beams, restored golden-pine paneling, and local rock exteriors are featured in this former "summer home" built in the 1930s. Located among tall pines near the west shore of Lake Tahoe, the b&b offers rooms decorated in a pleasing mixture of European and American antiques and Laura Ashley fabrics. Guest rooms feature large beds, down comforters, pillows, and sitting areas for in-room breakfasts, if desired. Two of the guest accommodations share a large bath with seven-foot Roman tub; pedestal sinks grace each room. The other rooms boast private, tiled baths. The full breakfast, featuring juice, muffins, croissants, and special entrees such as "Dutch Baby" or fruit crêpes, is served in the room, in the dining room, or on the terrace in the summer. Wine and cider are enjoyed by the cozy stone fireplace in the living room, as is late-night port and sherry. Guests also enjoy a large stone patio with outside fireplace in front of the inn.

Alpenhaus Country Inn

P.O. Box 262, 6941 West Lake Boulevard, Tahoma, CA 95733
Phone: (916) 525-5266
Key: Inn; 7 units; Moderate; Smoking OK; No children under 2;
Credit cards

This completely renovated inn with a fine European-style restaurant and bar boasts an Alpine decor and a swimming pool surrounded by trees and gardens. The interior of the inn features warm pine walls, Bavarian and Swiss imports, and bell-shaped-lantern light fixtures. The guest rooms, all with private baths, have pine- hand-painted headboards, cozy comforters, pine closets, and country wallpaper prints. Guests may enjoy a comfortable lounge with a small bar and rock fireplace. The full breakfast changes daily but might include omelettes, blueberry muffins, juice, and fresh fruit. The restaurant, featuring Swiss-Austrian cuisine, is open nightly.

Annie Horan's Bed & Breakfast, Grass Valley

Annie Horan's Bed & Breakfast

415 W. Main Street, Grass Valley, CA 95945
Phone: (916) 272-2418
Key: Inn; 4 units; Moderate; No smoking; No children under 15;
Credit cards

In terms of unique design and workmanship, this 1874 residence remains virtually unchanged since its early days. The interior of the inn, just a stroll away from Main Street shops, is decorated in antiques collected from Europe, the Orient, and all over the United States. The four guest rooms, all with private baths, are individually decorated, and the old parlor of the house is now a guest room with pretty Queen Anne furnishings. The dining room, with its original architecture, and a spacious deck are breakfast locales. The full breakfast includes a soufflé or egg dish, several types of pastry, fruit, juice, and coffee or tea.

Golden Ore House Bed & Breakfast

448 South Auburn Street, Grass Valley, CA 95945
Phone: (916) 272-6872
Key: Inn; 7 units; Inexpensive-Mod.; No smoking; No children under 12; Credit cards

This turn-of-the-century home with lots of charm is a short walk from the scenic Empire Mine State Park. The lovingly restored home is filled with fine antiques and abundant natural woodwork. It has two living rooms with fireplaces and an extra kitchen for guests, as well as a large second-story deck for lounging. The seven antique-decorated guest rooms include unusual attic rooms with skylights. A delicious, full breakfast, served in the dining room between 8:00 A.M. and 10:00 A.M., may include fruit, juice, muffins, eggs, waffles, and blintzes.

Golden Ore House Bed & Breakfast, Grass Valley

The Holbrooke Hotel

212 W. Main Street, Grass Valley, CA 95945
Phone: (916) 273-1353
Key: Inn/Hotel; 26 units; Inexpensive-Exp.; Limited smoking; No children under 13; Credit cards

This 130-year-old historic landmark in the center of Old Town is within walking distance to shops and historic sites. The meticulously restored hotel has an elegant dining room, which serves lunch and dinner, and the hotel's "Golden Gate Saloon" is the oldest continually operating saloon in the state. Each guest room is unique at the inn, although all are decorated in brass beds, claw-foot tubs, lace curtains, comforters, and turn-of-the-century antiques. Modern additions to rooms include color TV and telephone. This hotel offers guests a continental breakfast served in the parlor.

Murphy's Inn

318 Neal Street, Grass Valley, CA 95945
Phone: (916) 273-6873
Key: Inn; 8 units; Inexpensive-Mod.; No smoking; No children under 7; Credit cards

Originally this 1866 inn was the personal estate of a gold baron. Today the well-manicured Victorian sits within walking distance of town shops and restaurants. Guests may relax on the spacious veranda graced with ivy baskets, take a dip in the swimming spa, or enjoy a cozy fire in one of the sitting rooms. All but two of the guest rooms have private baths, and all are furnished in period pieces, lace curtains, antique brass beds, and floral wall coverings. A full breakfast awaits guest in the parlor or is presented in the room.

Purcell House

119 North Church Street, Grass Valley, CA 95945
Phone: (916) 272-5525
Key: Inn; 7 units; Inexpensive-Mod.; Limited smoking; No children; Credit cards

This inn was built in 1874 as a private residence and has been restored to recreate the same 1800s feel. All of the guest rooms have private baths with claw-foot tubs, pedestal sinks, and brass shower rings. The rooms are decorated authentically in antiques, wallpapers, and plump comforters, plus photographs of the mines they are named after. All rooms feature king- or queen-size beds. The freshly baked croissant, bread, and fresh-fruit breakfast is served in the parlor. The inn is now a part of the Holbrooke Hotel.

Swan-Levine House

328 South Church Street, Grass Valley, CA 95945
Phone: (916) 272-1873
Key: Inn; 4 units; Inexpensive-Mod.; No smoking; Children OK; Credit cards

The Victorian mansion, built before 1880, has been restored by the artist/owners. The main house features upstairs guest rooms, including one suite with private bath and parlor, others with oak bedsteads and wicker, and even a small room with bunkbeds for children. The carriage house has been renovated and is used as a printmaking studio. Reservations are required. Guests enjoy an outdoor pool surrounded by redwood decks and a tree-shaded yard.

The Harkey House

212 "C" Street, Yuba City, CA 95991
Phone: (916) 674-1942
Key: Home; 3 units; Moderate; Limited smoking; Children OK; No credit cards

This Victorian home, built in 1874, has three guest rooms. The "Harkey Suite" has a queen-size brass bed, wash basin, fireplace, and balcony; the "Yellow Wicker Room" features white-wicker decor, fresh flowers, and quilts. Besides breakfasting in the sunny dining room, guests may rent bikes for touring or enjoy the swimming pool and spa. Complimentary wine is served fireside. Recent additions to the b&b include a basketball court, a piano, and an art gallery.

Lincoln House Bed & Breakfast

191 Lincoln Way, Auburn, CA 95603
Phone: (916) 885-8880
Key: Home; 3 units; Inexpensive-Mod.; No smoking; No children under 11; No credit cards

Guests enter this storybook-style, 1933-built home by crossing a footbridge over koi-filled fish ponds. Terraces are surrounded by lush lawns, and a garden-lined swimming pool grants views of the Sierras and the American River canyon. The interior of the house is filled with soft pastel colors, family antiques, and se-

Lincoln House Bed & Breakfast, Auburn

lected 1930s and 1940s pieces. The three guest rooms, each with a private bath, are decorated in antiques, soft colors, and cozy quilts. Guests enjoy complimentary beverages each afternoon in the fireside sitting room and a homemade breakfast in the dining room with majestic views. The morning meal features such delectables as German pancakes, French toast, waffles, and homemade muffins.

Power's Mansion Inn

164 Cleveland Avenue, Auburn, CA 95603
Phone: (916) 885-1166
Key: Inn; 13 units; Moderate-Del.; Limited smoking; Children OK; Credit cards

Power's Mansion Inn, Auburn

This century-old Victorian mansion was built from a gold fortune and has been fully restored to its past elegance. The thirteen authentically decorated guest rooms at the inn boast private baths with brass and porcelain fixtures, air conditioning, big brass beds covered in satin comforters, windows trimmed in lace, and antique furniture. A full gourmet breakfast prepared by the innkeeper is served each morning. Gold-panning tours and special events are offered at this Victorian retreat.

The Victorian

195 Park Street, P.O. Box 9097, Auburn, CA 95604
Phone: (916) 885-5879
Key: Home; 3 units; Inexpensive-Mod.; No smoking; No children; No credit cards

This 134-year-old restored Victorian, two minutes from town, is situated on six acres atop a hill that offers spectacular views. The three guest rooms are beautifully furnished, and guests also enjoy a hot tub and swimming pool. A full breakfast is served in the morning and features waffles and a special bacon served on Royal Doulton china.

The American River Inn, Georgetown

The American River Inn

P.O. Box 43, Main at Orleans Street, Georgetown, CA 95634
Phone: (916) 333-4499
Key: Inn; 20 units; Moderate; Smoking OK; No children under 9; Credit cards.

This totally restored 1853 miners' boarding house and 1907 Queen Anne home is a former stagecoach stop nestled in the Sierra Nevada foothills. It offers guests strolls through Victorian gardens, a dove aviary, and a unique antique shop that can double as a guest room. Guests enjoy local wines in the parlor each evening and may relax in a refreshing, mountain-stream pool or the Jacuzzi. Bicycles are provided, as are picnic lunches on prior arrangement. The guest rooms at the inn feature turn-of-the-century decor and private as well as shared bath accommodations. A full breakfast is served in the dining room or on the patio. Games in the garden include croquet, badminton, Ping-Pong, and horseshoes; the inn is only ten minutes from white-water rafting, which the inn will arrange.

The Coloma Country Inn

P.O. Box 502, #2 High Street, Coloma, CA 95613
Phone: (916) 622-6919
Key: Inn; 5 units; Moderate; No smoking; No children under 6; Credit cards

Surrounded on all sides by history is this quiet house built in the 1850s. Sutter's Mill and pioneer churches sit alongside the inn, and many attractions, including the Marshall Gold Discovery Park and white-water rafting, are within walking distance of the gold-rush home. The inn has been carefully renovated, and the eleven rooms, including five guest rooms, are decorated in a pleasing combination of American antiques, primitives, quilts, and stenciling. The homemade breakfast, which includes muffins, fruit with whipped cream, and champagne, is served in the room or in the formal dining room. The inn offers spacial champagne–hot-air-ballooning tours over the American River valley.

Vineyard House

P.O. Box 176, Coloma CA 95613
Phone: (916) 622-2217
Key: Inn/Hotel; 7 units; Moderate; Smoking OK; No children; Credit cards

A famous vintner of the period built this four-story, 11,000-square-foot house in 1878. It consists of a ballroom, four dining rooms, a front parlor, old wine cellar, and jail cell (the latter two now form a saloon with entertainment). Guest rooms are upstairs, share a modern bath at the end of the hall, and are furnished in period pieces. Hotel guests are served a continental breakfast of homemade breads and jams and may also enjoy dinners in the public dining room. A guest lounge and gift shop are located on the premises.

The Chichester House

2908 Wood Street, Placerville, CA 95667
Phone: (916) 626-1882
Key: Inn; 3 units; Inexpensive-Mod.; No smoking; No children; No credit cards

A gold mine is hidden under the dining area of this lovingly restored 1892 Victorian home located on a hillside. California oaks, flower gardens, and a sixty-foot tulip tree surround the inn and its carriage house. The interior of the home features antique furnishings and a pump organ, and the library and parlor offer fireplaces and cozy reading nooks. The guest rooms are furnished in period pieces, and each has its own half bath. A full gourmet breakfast awaits guests each morning and features goodies such as eggs Benedict, German apple pancakes, crêpes, and quiche. Wine and sherry are offered in the afternoon.

Historic Combellack-Blair House

3059 Cedar Ravine, Placerville, CA 95667
Phone: (916) 622-3764
Key: Home; 2 units; Moderate; No smoking; No children; No credit cards

Built in 1895, this Queen Anne–Victorian home has been carefully restored and furnished in period decor with stained glass and antiques throughout. The two guest rooms share a bathroom. A full "country" breakfast of homemade English-muffin bread, jams, and country sausage begins each day, and afternoon brings complimentary refreshments and freshly baked goods in the parlor. Located in a quiet residential area, the b&b is within walking distance of the historic town of Placerville. The house is now on the National Register of Historic Places.

The Fleming Jones Homestead

3170 Newtown Road, Placerville, CA 95667
Phone: (916) 626-5840
Key: Inn; 6 units; Moderate; No smoking; Children under 12 on approval; No credit cards

The nineteenth-century farmhouse is surrounded by eleven acres of woods, flowers, and old mining sites in the Sierra foothills. The historic, two-story b&b has been restored, and the interior furnished in country antiques. The full breakfast, which includes eggs, homemade breads and preserves, fruit, and juice, is served at the large oak dining-room table. Treats are available in the parlor.

James Blair House

2985 Clay Street, Placerville, CA 95667
Phone: (916) 626-6136
Key: Inn; 4 units; Inexpensive-Mod.; No smoking; No children under 5; Credit cards

This 1901 Queen Anne features a three-story turret, stained-glass windows, a conservatory with skylights and beautiful woodwork. All guest rooms have queen-size beds; one has a private bath, one has a half bath, and two share a bath down the hall. A full breakfast is served in the fireside breakfast room. The innkeeper's displays of antique dolls and Chinese silk embroidery abound; lamps and lampshades are custom-made.

River Rock Inn, Placerville

River Rock Inn

1756 Georgetown Drive, P.O. Box 827, Placerville, CA 95667
Phone: (916) 622-7640
Key: Inn; 4 units; Moderate; Limited smoking; Children OK; No credit cards

129

Guests may fish or pan for gold in the front yard of this wood-and-glass inn faced with river rock. The river and trees provide the views from three of the rooms and the 140-foot deck that also offers a sunroom and hot tub. The interior of the comfortable inn is furnished in antiques and a country decor; guests enjoy the living room with TV and large fireplace. Breakfast, served in the dining room by fireside in the winter and in the sunroom in summer, features eggs Benedict or apple crêpes.

The Rupley House

2500 Highway 50, Placerville, CA 95667
Phone: (916) 626-0630
Key: Inn; 4 units; Moderate; No smoking; No children under 7; No credit cards

This 1929 Pennsylvania Dutch–style farmhouse is surrounded by one acre of estate gardens and fourteen acres of pastures. The country inn offers restful gardens, gold panning, and farm animals. The accommodations include three guest rooms with queen-size beds, one with twin beds, and one with private bath and balcony. The living room reflects the innkeepers' collection of Western–movie star collectibles and photos. The full breakfast may include such delectables as mammoth sourdough French toast with fresh fruit and homebaked muffins.

Sorensen's Resort

Highway 88, Hope Valley, CA 96120
Phone: (916) 694-2203
Key: Inn/Cottages; 20 units; Inexpensive-Exp.; No smoking; Children OK; Credit cards

This 165-acre resort in the High Sierra meadowland was founded by Danish sheepherders in 1893. The guest cabins are nestled in a grove of aspens, and each cabin is uniquely appointed with such details as fireplaces, cathedral ceilings, lofts, and kitchenettes. The continental breakfast, ordered from a reasonably priced menu, is an additional charge, but this bed & "hospitality"

130

establishment provides a complimentary glass of wine as well as coffee, tea, or hot cocoa throughout the day. Unlimited recreation at the resort includes volleyball, horseshoes, barbecues, two on-site creeks, and river rafting as well as trail-walking tours that include meals, lodging, and tour guides.

Partridge Inn

521 First Street, Davis, CA 95616
Phone: (916) 753-1211
Key: Inn; 7 units; Inexpensive-Mod.; No smoking; No children under 13; Credit cards

This gracious family mansion built in 1912 retains its original curved ceilings, brass fixtures, and pastel-glass chandeliers and is furnished in period pieces and family antiques. Guests gather in the high-ceilinged living room before a fire for wine and sherry and enjoy a generous breakfast buffet each morning. The guest rooms, all with private or semiprivate baths, are furnished in soft tones, warm antiques, and comforters, and several offer fireplaces. Bicycles are available at this inn convenient to city shops, restaurants, and the university

Amber House

1315 22nd Street, Sacramento, CA 95816
Phone: (916) 444-8085
Key: Inn; 4 units; Moderate; No smoking; No children; Credit cards

Framed by massive elms, this Craftsman-style inn in a residential area is touched with period elegance, such as beveled glass, boxed-beam ceilings, a clinker-brick fireplace, and hardwood floors. Guest rooms with rich burgundy carpeting, wallpapers, and antiques also offer stained-glass or French windows and private or semiprivate baths. A full gourmet breakfast including fresh fruit, a special entree, and homemade pastries is served in the formal dining room; wine and sherry are offered. Bikes are available, as is pickup service at the airport and train. Central air conditioning is featured in all the rooms at the inn.

Aunt Abigail's

2120 G Street, Sacramento, CA 95816
Phone: (916) 441-5007
Key: Inn; 5 units; Moderate; Limited smoking; Children over 15 on approval; Credit cards

This 1912 Colonial Revival mansion in the fashionable Boulevard Park area is framed by massive cedar and elm trees and boasts a former carriage area that is now a small park. The elegant interiors offer ten-foot-high ornate ceilings, antiques, and a warm, friendly feel. All five guest rooms have private baths, and many have brass beds, antique armoires, and Baroque porcelain sinks. The full breakfast, with award-winning coffee cakes and muffins, is served in the sunny dining room. Guests may relax in the spacious living room with fireplace, in the sitting room with its piano and games, or in the secluded, flower-filled garden.

The Bear Flag Inn

2814 I Street, Sacramento, CA 95816
Phone: (916) 448-5417
Key: Inn; 2 units; Moderate; Smoking OK; Children OK; Credit cards

This European-style hostelry is in a downtown residential area just two blocks from Sutter's Fort. The restored California Arts and Crafts bungalow offers guest rooms with private baths furnished in period pieces, William Morris–designed wallcoverings, and carved double beds. Guests enjoy a decanter of wine and books in the room as well as a living room with piano and fireplace. The continental breakfast includes croissants and grapefruit from the garden.

The Briggs House

2209 Capitol Avenue, Sacramento, CA 95816
Phone: (916) 441-3214

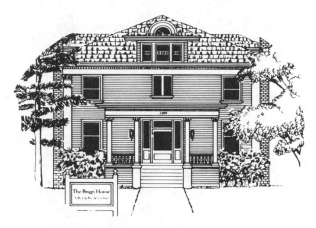

The Briggs House, Sacramento

Key: Inn/Cottage; 7 units; Moderate-Exp.; No smoking; Children on approval; Credit cards

This elegantly restored Victorian surrounded by stately trees is furnished in European and American antiques, rich wood paneling, inlaid hardwood floors, oriental rugs, and lace curtains. Accommodations include a second-story carriage house with teddy bears, kitchenette, and bath as well as guest rooms in the house that feature some fireplaces, claw-foot tubs, and sun porches. Coffee, juice, and a gourmet breakfast are served in the garden or in the room. A sauna, spa, and bicycles are for guests' use.

The Driver Mansion Inn

2019 21st Street, Sacramento, CA 95818
Phone: (916) 455-5243
Key: Inn; 10 units; Moderate-Del.; No smoking; No children; Credit cards

A high degree of care has gone into preserving this 1899 family mansion with corner tower in the heart of downtown. A sweeping staircase and stately entry lead to the parlor and dining

133

The Driver Mansion Inn, Sacramento

room with leaded glass, fireplaces, and a refinished 1907 grand piano. The guest rooms, spacious and beautifully appointed in unusual walnut and mahogany pieces, original art, rare Victorian lighting, and oriental carpets, have private marble tiled baths with Victorian fixtures. All guest rooms feature such modern touches as wall-to-wall carpeting, private phones, and central air and heat. The inn features deluxe master suites with spas and a restored carriage house boasting fireplaces and Jacuzzis.

Morning Glory

700 22nd Street, Sacramento, CA 95816
Phone: (916) 447-7829
Key: Inn; 5 units; Inexpensive-Mod.; No smoking; Children on arrangement; Credit cards

A Colonial Revival built in 1906, this inn is appointed with dark-stained woodwork and window seats plus beveled-glass windows and brass lighting fixtures. Guest rooms, all with private baths, are decorated in antiques, lace curtains, memorabilia, armoires, carpeting, and quaint wall coverings. A solarium and parlor with piano are available to guests. The always special breakfast can include baked apples, quiche, sourdough French toast, or banana pecan waffles. Late-afternoon wine and beverages are served.

The Mine House Inn

P.O. Box 245, Amador City, CA 95601
Phone: (209) 267-5900
Key: Inn; 8 units; Inexpensive-Mod.; Smoking OK; Children OK;
No credit cards

This most unusual hostelry is the one-hundred-year-old former Keystone Consolidated Mining Office Building, and each guest room is named after its original use: the "Mill Grinding Room" with the original shaft supporters, the "Vault Room" with the original bullion safe, and so on. Guests enjoy a swimming pool, a sitting room, and an art gallery/gift shop. A complete continental breakfast consisting of orange juice, breakfast rolls, and coffee, tea, or hot chocolate is served to each guest in the morning.

Botto Country Inn

11 Sutter Hill Road, Sutter Creek, CA 95685
Phone: (209) 267-5519
Key: Inn; 5 units; Moderate; Limited smoking; Children on approval; Credit cards

The inn, built originally in 1860 as a residence, has a country setting on more than one acre of lawn and pastures one-quarter mile from downtown. Guests may enjoy the tranquility from the upstairs and downstairs porches. The individually decorated guest rooms with country wallpaper and antiques share two baths with claw-foot tubs. A full, homemade breakfast is served in the dining room each morning and features fresh fruit with sherbet, herb scrambled eggs with sauteed vegetables, brown potatoes with onions, ham with orange sauce, and sauteed apples, all served by candlelight.

The Foxes in Sutter Creek

P.O. Box 159, 77 Main Street, Sutter Creek, CA 95685
Phone: (209) 267-5882

Key: Inn; 6 units; Moderate-Exp.; No smoking; No children; Credit cards

This inn occupies a building that also houses a real estate office and personal residence; it was built in 1857 during the gold-rush days. Accommodations include suites that are furnished in specially selected antiques and have dining and sitting areas as well as private baths, queen-size beds, and air conditioning. The remodeled downstairs suite boasts a fireplace and large bath with crystal chandelier and claw-foot tub, as well as a private entrance and porch. Three accommodations at the inn boast fireplaces. The bountiful country breakfast is served on a silver service, along with the morning newspaper, in the suite or on the tree-roofed gazebo surrounded by colorful azaleas. Guests enjoy covered parking and courtesy pick-up at the airport.

The Hanford House

P.O. Box 847, 3 Hanford Street, Sutter Creek, CA 95685
Phone: (209) 267-0747
Key: Inn; 9 units; Moderate-Exp; No smoking; No children under 15; Credit cards

The inn is a new, brick structure built around a Spanish cottage and is reminiscent of a turn-of-the-century San Francisco warehouse. In the same way, the furnishings at the b&b blend both the old and new with a country feel. All of the guest rooms offer private baths and ceiling fans and are bright and spacious. The suite features a fireplace. Guests relax on a seventy-three-foot redwood deck that affords breathtaking views of the countryside. A complimentary bottle of wine comes with each room, and the inn serves a hearty continental breakfast.

Nancy & Bob's Nine Eureka Street Inn

#9 Eureka Street, P.O. Box 386, Sutter Creek, CA 95685
Phone: (209) 267-0342
Key: Inn; 5 units; Moderate; No smoking; No children; Credit cards

The 1916 inn, just two blocks from town shops, has rich woods, stained-glass windows, and antique furnishings. All five guest rooms feature private baths, air conditioning, and queen-size beds. The sitting room is for guests' enjoyment, and a full breakfast greets guests each morning in the sunny dining room.

Sutter Creek Inn

75 Main Street, P.O. Box 385, Sutter Creek, CA 95685
Phone: (209) 267-5606
Key: Inn/Cottages; 19 units; Inexpensive-Mod.; Limited smoking; No children; No credit cards

The 1859-built inn, the biggest house in town, offers accommodations upstairs and in several outbuildings in the rear of the house that have been totally refurbished. The unusual colors and eclectic decorating schemes include swinging beds (which can be stabilized), fireplaces, Franklin stoves, canopies, and brightly colored wicker. Guests may relax in the living room or on outside hammocks. An imaginative country breakfast is prepared and served in the spacious old kitchen. Handwriting analysis is done upon request at this hospitable inn, as are professional massages or relexology.

The Heirloom

214 Shakeley Lane, P.O. Box 322, Ione, CA 95640
Phone: (209) 274-4468
Key: Inn; 6 units; Inexpensive-Mod.; Smoking OK; No children under 11; No credit cards

The home of one of the earliest settlers in the Ione Valley, this Greek Revival structure is situated on nearly two acres of secluded grounds. The private grounds, full of ancient trees, shrubs, and gardens, provide lawns for croquet, a gazebo, and hammocks, as well as umbrella tables and swings. Guests may relax in the living room of the house with its fireplace and ten-foot-high ceilings and in the dining room with a crystal chandelier and fireplace. The rooms are all furnished with family heirlooms and

137

antiques; several of the guest rooms boast balconies or fireplaces. Afternoon refreshments are served, and a full breakfast is served in bed, on the balcony, in the garden, or in the dining room.

Ann Marie's Country Inn

410 Stasal Street, Jackson, CA 95642
Phone: (209) 223-1452
Key: Inn/Cottage; 5 units; Moderate; Limited smoking; Children OK; Credit cards

This authentic country Victorian with bay windows was constructed in 1892 during the gold-mining days. The guest rooms are full of quality antiques and are decorated with wallpaper prints and old lace and linens. Two of the accommodations have brass beds; a separate cottage is a romantic retreat with queen-size brass bed, potbelly stove, and bath. Guests enjoy a parlor with games, a Victorian-style wood-burning stove, and music, as well as complimentary beverages. A full "harvest" breakfast of perhaps eggs Benedict, omelettes, or quiche with fried potatoes and fresh fruit is served at 9:00 A.M. each morning. Babysitting is available at this inn, which welcomes children.

Broadway Hotel

225 Broadway, Jackson, CA 95642
Phone: (209) 223-3503
Key: Inn/Hotel; 15 units; Inexpensive; Smoking OK; Children OK; Credit cards

From the gold-rush days through 1942, the hotel served as a haven for miners. Today, the b&b inn captures days gone by with its restored guest rooms, most with private bath, air conditioning, and bright, airy colors. The "summer hospitality hour" includes sherry and cheeses for enjoyment in the garden, gazebo, covered Jacuzzi, or dining room. Breakfasts of prize-winning nut breads and a fresh-fruit bowl greet guests.

Court Street Inn, Jackson

Court Street Inn

215 Court Street, Jackson, CA 95642
Phone: (209) 223-0416
Key: Inn; 6 units; Moderate-Exp.; Smoking OK; No children under 13; No credit cards

The fully restored 1870 Mother Lode home is listed on the National Register of Historic Places. Fine antiques, lace curtains, and abundant fresh flowers are some of the special touches. Guest accommodations include two deluxe suites with two guest rooms, private bath, living room, and (in one) fireplace. Other guest rooms feature specially selected antiques, one with French doors leading to a private deck. Guests may relax on the large porch with wicker furniture while enjoying complimentary wine. A full breakfast is served in the room or on the patio and features eggs Benedict, French toast, crêpes, waffles, or soufflés.

The Gate House Inn

1330 Jackson Gate Road, Jackson, CA 95642
Phone: (209) 223-3500
Key: Inn/Cottage; 5 units; Moderate-Exp.; No smoking; No children; No credit cards

139

The Victorian inn and separate summerhouse are a step into the past created with antiques, lace curtains, and handmade afghans. Guest rooms in the house all have private baths and brass or early American queen-size beds. The summerhouse's two-room suite offers a wood-burning stove and bath with claw-foot tub and pull-chain toilet. Guests are invited to relax on the porches and in the picnic area and to enjoy the swimming pool. A full breakfast in the formal dining room is served on fine china.

The Robin's Nest, San Andreas

The Robin's Nest—A Country Inn

P.O. Box 1408, 247 W. St. Charles Street, San Andreas, CA 95249
Phone: (209) 754-1076
Key: Inn; 9 units; Moderate; Smoking OK; No children under 13; No credit cards

This relaxed country estate consists of an 1845 Queen Anne–Victorian home with views of the Sierra foothills and charming gardens. The spacious inn, within walking distance of shops and restaurants, features a large parlor, sitting room, dining room, and music room with antique pump organ and grand piano. An extensive library is available as well as a TV. The guest rooms are named and decorated after turn-of-the-century modes of transportation. The "Buggy Room" is a gabled suite with a seventeen-foot-high ceiling and views of the countryside. Breakfast is served buffet style and includes such items as quiches, crêpes, and frittatas; champagne is offered. Iced tea and wine are served on arrival; after-dinner coffee and brandy are offered. This creative inn offers many specialty weekends including innovative mystery weekends with guest participation and country-western weekends with shoot-outs, barbecues, and country breakfasts.

Dunbar House

P.O. Box 1375, 271 Jones Street, Murphys, CA 95247
Phone: (209) 728-2897
Key: Inn; 5 units; Moderate; No smoking; No children under 10; Credit cards

The 1880 restored Italianate-style home was used as a location site for the TV series "Seven Brides for Seven Brothers." Calaveras County's first b&b blends old and new comforts in its guest accommodations with electric blankets and air conditioning, and features family antiques, laces, and light, cheery wall coverings throughout. Wine, books, and games await guests in the parlor, and a full breakfast is served fireside in the dining room, on the porch, or in the gardens. Future plans include a putting green.

City Hotel

P.O. Box 1870, Columbia, CA 95310
Phone: (209) 532-1479
Key: Inn/Hotel; 9 units; Moderate; Limited smoking; Children OK; Credit cards

A part of the Columbia Historic State Park, a historic 1800s town, this hotel is a combined living museum, training center for hotel management, restaurant, and b&b establishment. Each luxuriously appointed guest room, with balcony or sitting area, has a private half bath and authentic antiques. Overnight lodging includes a continental breakfast each morning. Other meals are available in the restaurant Tuesday through Sunday.

Fallon Hotel

P.O. Box 1870, Washington Street, Columbia, CA 95310
Phone: (209) 532-1470
Key: Inn/Hotel; 14 units; Inexpensive-Exp.; Limited smoking; Children OK; Credit cards

The state of California finished restoration of the 1857-built Fallon Hotel in the historic park of Columbia in 1986. The lodging establishment with brick facade and wooden balcony is a "living museum," boasting many of its original furnishings and other antiques as well as authentic wallpaper reproductions that return it to its Victorian grandeur. Most of the guest rooms offer half baths and share showers, and accommodations range from the intimate hall rooms to the elaborate "Bridal Suite." Five rooms open onto the balcony for a birds's-eye view of the charming town. The complimentary breakfast includes fresh breads, sweet rolls, juices, and coffee or tea and is served to guests only in the parlor on the first floor. The hotel participates in a number of special events year-round and offers special lodging, dinner, and theater packages. The Fallon is partially staffed by hospitality-management students from Columbia College.

Twain Harte's Bed & Breakfast

18864 Manzanita Drive, Box 1718, Twain Harte, CA 95383
Phone: (209) 586-3311
Key: Inn; 6 units; Inexpensive-Mod.; Smoking OK; Children OK; Credit cards

This b&b with lots of decks and walkways is situated in a wooded setting yet is within walking distance of downtown. Each of the guest rooms has its own decor and sink. One guest accommodation boasts private bath, and another offers a complete family suite with living room and bath. Guests enjoy a cozy living room with fireplace and antiques, a recreation room with pool table and bar, and a breakfast room, where the country-style breakfast is served. Excellent restaurants are within walking distance.

Barretta Gardens Inn

700 So. Barretta Street, Sonora, CA 95370
Phone: (209) 532-6039
Key: Inn; 4 units; Moderate; No smoking; No children under 15 or on approval; Credit cards

The 1904 inn offers guest rooms with queen-size beds, shared baths (except one private-bath accommodation on the first floor), antiques, and color schemes that complement the flowers in the gardens. Complimentary beverages are served each evening and may be enjoyed in the three guest parlors and on the sun porch or the wraparound porch. The full breakfast is accompanied by classical or easy-listening music performed by the guitarist-innkeeper and is served in the dining room, breakfast room, or on the front porch. The inn is located on one acre of terraced gardens and is within walking distance of downtown.

Gunn House

286 South Washington Street, Sonora, CA 95370
Phone: (209) 532-3421
Key: Inn/Hotel; 25 units; Inexpensive-Mod.; Smoking OK; Children OK; Credit cards

This 1850 residence was the first two-story adobe built in Sonora. The original adobe makes up the core of the restored hotel. All of the guest rooms are decorated in priceless antiques but have the modern conveniences of electric heat, air conditioning, and television. Guests enjoy a pleasant patio area and a heated swimming pool. A continental breakfast is served each morning, and cocktails are available in the "Josephine Room."

Jameson's

22157 Feather River Drive, Sonora, CA 95370
Phone: (209) 532-1248
Key: Inn; 4 units; Inexpensive-Mod.; Limited smoking; No children; No credit cards

Nestled among four acres of oaks and boulders is this redwood-and-glass house that straddles a creek and boasts natural waterfalls front and rear. The four guest rooms, some with their own wooden deck, and spacious and decorated in a "lady" theme from songs or stories. The "Scheherazade" room has an exotic, draped bed with Arabian beads, screens, and brass. Guests enjoy a high-ceilinged living room with fireplace and a game room with a pool table. The extended continental breakfast with homemade scones, Irish soda bread, or other oven-fresh treats is offered each morning.

The Ryan House, Sonora

The Ryan House

153 So. Shepherd Street, Sonora, CA 95370
Phone: (209) 533-3445
Key: Inn; 4 units; Inexpensive-Mod.; No smoking; Children on approval; Credit cards

This gold-rush home, built in the 1850s and winner of a historic-preservation award, is framed by lovely rose gardens and is within walking distance of town. Guest rooms are furnished in antiques and antique reproductions and a constant supply of fresh flowers from the garden. The full breakfast with such specialties as banana-walnut pancakes or chili egg puff along with homemade breads is served each morning. Guests are invited to relax in front of the fire at the end of the day.

Serenity

15305 Bear Cub Drive, P.O. Box 3484, Sonora, CA 95370
Phone: (209) 533-1441
Key: Inn; 4 units; Moderate; Smoking OK; No children; Credit cards

This period home nestled in the pines offers uniquely decorated rooms with many handmade items. Each room has its own bath and either a queen-size or twin beds. Fireside refreshments are served in the "Commons" or on the veranda each evening, and a hearty breakfast featuring homemade preserves is offered in the dining room. Guests are invited to enjoy the piano, game table, or library, which features mother-lode reading material.

Jamestown Hotel

P.O. Box 539, Jamestown, CA 95327
Phone: (209) 984-3902
Key: Inn/Hotel; 8 units; Moderate; Smoking OK; Children OK; Credit cards

This historic hotel with adjoining restaurant and saloon offers rooms and suites that have been restored to reflect the gold-rush period and the early days of the Sierra Railroad. All accommodations have private Victorian baths and antiques, and some have separate sitting rooms. Guests are invited to relax or sunbathe on the outdoor deck. A continental breakfast is served each morning.

Royal Hotel

18239 Main Street, P.O. Box 219, Jamestown, CA 95327
Phone: (209) 984-5271
Key: Inn/Hotel/Cottage; 19 units; Inexpensive-Mod.; Smoking OK; Children OK; Credit cards

This hotel in historic Jamestown was built in 1922. The gold-mining town has been the locale of many movies and TV series.

Victorian-style guest rooms are in the main building, and a honeymoon cottage is in the rear. Guests are encouraged to use the patio, gas barbecues, gazebo, and old-fashioned balconies. A continental breakfast is served each morning. Senior citizens enjoy a discount on weekdays.

Oak Hill Ranch

P.O. Box 307, 18550 Connally Lane, Tuolumne, CA 95379
Phone: (209) 928-4717
Key: Inn/Cottage; 4 units; Moderate; No smoking; No children under 15; No credit cards

This rural Victorian ranch house with cottage sits on fifty-five acres and looks out onto pastures, ponds, and the Sierras. The house guest rooms have been carefully restored and are authentically decorated in antiques. These accommodations feature two rooms with private baths and two with shared baths that boast claw-foot tubs. The "Cow Palace" cottage, also in antiques, is totally private; has a rock fireplace, two queen beds, and a furnished kitchen; and may accommodate groups. A full gourmet breakfast featuring such dishes as Normandy crêpes, crunchy French toast, or "Eggs Fantasia" is served in the dining room; prebreakfast coffee, in the old-fashioned gazebo.

Dick and Shirl's

4870 Triangle Road, Mariposa, CA 95338
Phone: (209) 966-2514
Key: Home; 1 unit; Inexpensive; Smoking OK; Children OK; No credit cards

This b&b home offers a quiet country setting surrounded by pines for travelers on their way to Yosemite National Park. The single guest accommodation with private bath also includes a full breakfast each morning served in the dining room or on the patio.

Granny's Garden

7333 Highway 49 North, Mariposa, CA 95338
Phone: (209) 377-8342
Key: Home; 3 units; Inexpensive-Mod.; Limited smoking; No children; Credit cards

This small Victorian farmhouse near Yosemite National Park boasts a large garden area with more than one hundred rose bushes and fresh produce. The 1896 inn is decorated in comfortable antiques; the main floor offers two bedrooms, and the upstairs is a private suite. A generous morning meal is served on the sunporch or in the dining room. A cellar porch with seven-foot skylights is decorated with kitchen and mining utensils. This cheerful, and homey air-conditioned inn is open May through October but closed in the winter due to lack of central heating.

Meadow Creek Ranch

2669 Triangle Road, Mariposa, CA 95338
Phone: (209) 966-3843
Key: Inn; 4 units; Moderate; No smoking; No children under 12; Credit cards

This original 1858 overnight stagecoach stop is on eight acres of land and contains the main two-story ranch house and bran cottage. Innkeepers greet guests with refreshments and encourage them to take a relaxing stroll around the grounds. The four comfortable guest rooms have European and country antiques, original art, and lots of plants. The "Country Cottage" room offers a private bath, kitchenette, and queen-size canopy bed. The full breakfast is served family style in the dining room or on the patio.

The Pelennor

3871 Highway 49 South, Mariposa, CA 95338
Phone: (209) 966-2832
Key: Home; 4 units; Inexpensive; Limited smoking; Children OK;
No credit cards

This hospitable b&b with a Scottish theme offers a new two-story b&b building with two baths and a common room as well as two rooms in the innkeeper's adjoining home. The fifteen-acre country setting offers serenity and pretty gardens. The decor is basic but features some tartan touches; the innkeepers will play a few tunes on the bagpipes upon request. A full breakfast with an egg dish, a meat, muffins, croissants, homemade breads, juice, cereal, and fruits will satisfy any appetite. New plans include a lap pool, spa, sauna house, and jogging path; the property plans to accommodate weddings.

SAN FRANCISCO BAY AREA

To Tomales To Santa Rosa   To Napa   To Sacramento

1
Inverness   101   37   29   80   680
NOVATO   VALLEJO

Point Reyes
Station
Olema   Benicia

SAN RAFAEL   4   4

1   80   CONCORD
Larkspur   17   Point Richmond
Bolinas   BERKELEY   Walnut Creek

Muir Beach   24
Sausalito   OAKLAND
80   680

SAN FRANCISCO   ALAMEDA
280   17
101   580   580
HAYWARD
Pleasanton

LEGEND:
—— Freeway Route
—— Highway Route   **Burlingame** 92
⌀ Listed City or Town   17   680
○ Location Reference   280
○LARGER CITY   1   84

Half Moon Bay

237   17
NORTH   Sunnyvale
Scale in Miles   SAN JOSE
0   5   10   15   20   To Davenport

SAN FRANCISCO BAY AREA   To Los Gatos 101

Synonymous with Fisherman's Wharf, cable cars, and China-town, the City also offers numerous cultural activities, fine res-taurants, and splendid examples of Victorian architecture blended with the ultramodern edifices. The communities that surround San Francisco, all just minutes away, bring suburban and country settings. Nearby Berkeley reflects the University of California campus with small coffee houses and boutiques, as well as stately homes. The suburban communities of Sunnyvale and Los Gatos are home to commuters, but each has retained its own identity. Just over the Golden Gate Bridge lies Sausalito with its hillside homes perched over the bay and its many tourist shops and art galleries. Over by the coast, but still within a modest drive, are communities such as Muir Beach, Tomales Bay, Olema, Point Reyes, and Inverness. They offer forests with hiking, seafood stops, beautiful beaches, and wilderness areas.

Byron Randall's Famous Victorian Tomales Guest House

P.O. Box 37, 25 Valley Street, Tomales, CA 94971
Phone: (707) 878-9992
Key: Inn; 8 units; Inexpensive-Mod.; Smoking OK; No children under 10; No credit cards

This rustic redwood Victorian surrounded by trees, gardens, and lily ponds offers a do-it-yourself approach to b&b travel. Guests check themselves in and out here, are urged to use the kitchen, and may never see the innkeeper. The decor is an inter-esting mixture of unique collectibles and the owner's own art. Breads, juice, and coffee constitute the self-serve breakfast. Guests may relax in the spacious social room with library, game table, and fireplace.

The Ark

P.O. Box 273, #180 Highland Way, Inverness, CA 94937
Phone: (415) 663-8276
Key: Cottage; 1 unit; Moderate-Exp.; Smoking OK; Children OK; No credit cards

150

A one-mile walk up the ridge from Inverness is this two-room artist's retreat nestled in the forest. The spacious main room boasts a cathedral ceiling, sunny forest-view windows, a wood stove, queen-size bed, and sleeping loft with futon. A smaller room adorned with the artwork of past visitors offers twin beds, a tape deck and stereo, and reading material. The cottage offers both toilet and sink, but guests bathe "Japanese style" in a separate octagonal shower and bath house with big Victorian tub and skylights. The full kitchen is stocked with breakfast fixings of eggs, juice, fresh fruit, granola, pastries, scones or muffins, braided egg bread, and homemade jams. A few steps outside the cottage waits an area for picnics and barbecues.

Blackthorne Inn

P.O. Box 712, 266 Vallejo Avenue, Inverness, CA 94937
Phone: (415) 663-8621
Key: Inn; 5 units; Moderate-Exp.; Limited smoking; No children; Credit cards

The multilevel wood-and-glass inn resembles a tree house nestled in a rustic, tree-filled canyon. Guest rooms perched from top floor to bottom yield views as well as added privacy and lead to a deck offering spectacular views and a hot tub for guests' use. An A-frame living room is for guests' enjoyment, as is a 3,000-square-foot sun deck. A buffet breakfast consisting of quiche, coffee cakes, juice, and fresh fruit salad with toppings is served at 9:30 A.M.

The MacLean House

P.O. Box 651, Inverness, CA 94937
Phone: (415) 669-7392
Key: Home; 3 units; Moderate; No smoking; No children under 6; No credit cards

This small inn overlooking Tomales Bay is situated among many trees to provide a relaxing retreat. The "Scottish" hostelry offers private baths in all rooms as well as private patios. The

151

morning continental breakfast consists of fresh fruit and home-made pastries. Complimentary sherry and shortbread are offered at this home filled with family tartan and antiques.

Rosemary Cottage

P.O. Box 619, 75 Balboa Avenue, Inverness, CA 94937
Phone: (415) 663-9338
Key: Cottage; 1 unit; Moderate-Exp.; Smoking OK; Children OK; No credit cards

Located on Inverness Ridge is this French country cottage with hand-crafted cabinets and tile. The b&b offers a large bedroom with queen-size bed; a main room with high ceilings, wood-burning stove, and picture-window views of the forest; additional sleeping areas; a full kitchen; and a bath with tub and shower. A full breakfast of juice, seasonal fruit, granola, fresh eggs (guests cook their own), pastries or muffins, and sometimes hot crêpes is offered each morning. A large deck nestled under an old oak overlooks the herb garden at this secluded getaway near Point Reyes National Seashore and Tomales Bay.

Holly Tree Inn, Point Reyes Station

Ten Inverness Way, Inverness

Ten Inverness Way

10 Inverness Way, P.O. Box 63, Inverness, CA 94937
Phone: (415) 669-1648
Key: Inn; 4 units; Moderate-Exp.; Limited smoking; Children on
approval; Credit cards

This 1904 guest house near Point Reyes National Seashore is
surrounded by a colorful garden and fruit trees. Sloped-ceiling
rooms with antiques and private baths and a living room with a
huge stone fireplace await guests. The full breakfast specialties
include banana or blackberry pancakes.

Holly Tree Inn

P.O. Box 642, 3 Silverhills Road, Point Reyes Station, CA 94956
Phone: (415) 663-1554
Key: Inn/Cottage; 5 units; Moderate-Exp.; Limited smoking; Chil-
dren OK; Credit cards

This b&b inn is located on nineteen acres of land and is surrounded by fir, bay, and oak trees; fragrant gardens; lilacs in the spring; and festive holly trees just in time for Christmas. The 4,000-square-foot inn with beamed ceilings and fireplaces offers four guest rooms, a living room with fireplace and comfortable seating, and a dining room, as well as a back deck that joins a hillside draped in heather. The guest accommodations offer plush carpeting, antique furnishings, Laura Ashley prints, garden views, and private baths. The generous country breakfast of farm-fresh eggs, homemade poppy-seed bread, juice, and fruit is served by the cozy curved hearth in the dining room. Wine and sherry are served in the afternoon. The inn offers a new cottage with privacy and views of the gardens, creek, and forest. The cottage boasts a sitting room/library, wood-burning stove, king-size bed, kitchenette (for self-serve breakfast), bath with claw-foot tub, and patio.

Thirty-Nine Cypress

P.O. Box 176, Point Reyes Station, CA 94956
Phone: (415) 663-1709
Key: Home; 3 units; Moderate; No smoking; No children; No credit cards

Situated on a bluff above Tomales Bay, this home offers views of cattle grazing and evergreen hills. Each of the guest rooms, which share one bath, is furnished in family antiques, oriental rugs, and original works of art. Guests are offered a glass of wine on the patio as well as a full breakfast each morning.

Bear Valley Bed & Breakfast

P.O. Box 33, 88 Bear Valley Road, Olema, CA 94950
Phone: (415) 663-1777
Key: Home; 3 units; Moderate; No smoking; No children; Credit cards (AE only)

This two-story Victorian ranch house is just one-half mile from Point Reyes National Park, which offers many recreational activities and exhibits. The 1899-built inn is surrounded by gardens and fruit orchards and offers guests a relaxing living room with oak floors, wallpaper, overstuffed seating, and cozy woodstove. The three individually furnished guest accommodations include some family antiques and a shared bath with the ranch's original claw-foot tub. A typical breakfast here might offer quiche, juice, homebaked muffins, and coffee or tea.

East Brother Light Station

117 Park Place, Point Richmond, CA 94801
Phone: (415) 233-2385
Key: Inn; 4 units; Deluxe; Limited smoking; No children; No credit cards

A unique b&b accommodation, this restored 1874 lighthouse station offers a total package of overnight lodging, continental breakfast, dinner with wine, and boat transportation from the yacht harbor to the island. The entire station, on the National Register of Historic Places, serves as a living museum of American maritime history and offers many Victorian buildings to explore.

The Panama Hotel & Cafe

4 Bayview Street, San Rafael, CA 94901
Phone: (415) 457-3993
Key: Inn/Hotel; 15 units; Inexpensive-Mod.; Smoking OK; Children OK; Credit cards

The urban inn is situated in the central shopping area of town. Accommodations include cozy rooms, many with balconies and more than half with private bath. Rates include a full breakfast served in the room or in the café, which is open daily and serves light meals, wine, and imported beers.

The Pelican Inn

Muir Beach, CA 94965
Phone: (415) 383-6000
Key: Inn; 6 units; Expensive; Smoking OK; Children OK; Credit cards

This Tudor-style farmhouse with pub and restaurant captures the spirit of sixteenth-century England yet is just twenty minutes from San Francisco. English antiques, a hearty English breakfast, and British ales, fine ports, wine, and tea carry out the theme. Luncheon service is available Tuesday through Saturday; a Sunday buffet lunch and dinner are also available. Lodging reservations are taken from 9:30 A.M. to 4:30 P.M.

Casa Madrona Hotel & Restaurant

801 Bridgeway, Sausalito, CA 94965
Phone: (415) 332-7296
Key: Inn/Hotel/Cottages; 32 units; Moderate-Del.; Smoking OK; Children OK; Credit cards

This historic 1885 Victorian is located fifteen minutes north of San Francisco across the Golden Gate Bridge. Situated on a hillside overlooking the harbor, the hotel is within walking distance of quaint town shops. Guest accommodations, located in the main house as well as in cottages, include sixteen modern, designer-decorated rooms with views. The award-winning restaurant at the inn features American cuisine, and guests enjoy a complimentary continental breakfast. Guests may also use the private Jacuzzi.

Sausalito Hotel

16 El Portal, Sausalito, CA 94965
Phone: (415) 332-4155
Key: Inn/Hotel; 14 units; Moderate-Del.; Smoking OK; No children under 8; Credit cards

Located in the downtown area, this historic hotel offers free parking to its guests. All of the guest rooms are decorated in antiques, but most notable is the "Marquis de Queensbury Room," which allows occupants to sleep in General Ulysses Grant's bed by fireside. A continental breakfast is included.

The Abigail Hotel

246 McAllister Street, San Francisco, CA 94102
Phone: (415) 861-9728
Key: Inn/Hotel; 9 units; Moderate; Smoking OK; Children OK; Credit cards

Located in the Civic Center area of the city, this restored hotel blends English country-inn qualities with modern conveniences. Each room contains color TV, phone, and a private, modern bath as well as turn-of-the-century antiques. The restaurant at the hotel serves complimentary breakfast and afternoon tea and offers luncheon.

Alamo Square Inn

719 Scott Street, San Francisco, CA 94117
Phone: (415) 922-2055
Key: Inn; 8 units; Moderate-Del.; Limited smoking; No children under 11; Credit cards

This large 1895 Queen Anne–Victorian b&b overlooks Alamo Square and the city skyline. Oak floors, a grand staircase, period decor, and oriental accents create an elegant setting for this b&b. Guest accommodations range from intimate double rooms to deluxe suites with both private and shared baths. Telephones are available in all rooms, and parking is available on the premises. The garden complex also offers several common rooms with fireplaces, where guests may linger over late-afternoon wine and snacks or evening sherry. The hearty continental breakfast includes homebaked breads prepared by the resident chef. Catered dinners are available on arrangement.

Albion House

135 Gough Street, San Francisco, CA 94102
Phone: (415) 621-0896
Key: Inn; 8 units; Moderate-Exp.; Smoking OK; Children OK;
Credit cards

Built after the great earthquake of 1906, the inn near Symphony Hall has gone through many periods of decor. The three-story building hosts a restaurant on the bottom floor and the b&b inn on the two upper levels. Each guest room offers a combination of Victorian, oriental, and Californian decor and features many carved wooden antiques and brass beds. Several guest rooms have private sun decks, and all have private baths. Sherry is served fireside in the spacious living room, and breakfast in the dining room includes croissants, boiled eggs, fresh fruit, and juice.

The Andrews Hotel

624 Post Street, San Francisco, CA 94109
Phone: (415) 563-6877 / (800) 227-4742 / (800) 622-0557 (CA)
Key: Inn/Hotel; 48 units; Moderate-Exp.; Smoking OK; Children OK; Credit cards

Furnished in original antiques, European lace curtains, and exotic plants, this elegant and gracious Victorian hotel also offers color TV, modern baths, and telephones in each room. Fresh fruit, baked goods, and coffee or tea is served on each floor in the morning. The inn is within walking distance of restaurants, stores, and theaters and two blocks from Union Square.

The Archbishops Mansion Inn

1000 Fulton Street, San Francisco, CA 94117
Phone: (415) 563-7872
Key: Inn; 13 units; Expensive-Del.; Limited smoking; No children under 13; Credit cards

Built for the archbishop of San Francisco in 1904, this elegantly restored mansion with open, carved mahogany staircase, stained-glass dome, and spacious country-manor guest suites is a luxurious b&b offering. The guest rooms, all with carved queen-size beds, private baths, sitting areas, and fireplaces, are filled with oriental carpets, museum-quality French antiques, canopies, oil paintings, and period chandeliers. As a salute to the nearby opera house, each guest room is named after a nineteenth-century opera. Guests gather for wine tastings in the late afternoon, and a French picnic basket packed with gourmet croissants, jams, juice, and beverages is delivered to the room at guests' specified time each morning. Limousine service is provided on special occasions for the pampered guests of this b&b mansion.

Art Center Bed & Breakfast, San Francisco

Art Center Bed & Breakfast

1902 Filbert Street, San Francisco, CA 94123
Phone: (415) 567-1526
Key: Inn; 4 units; Moderate-Exp.; No smoking; Children OK; Credit cards

Constructed in 1857 on a fresh-water lagoon that was used as a washerwoman's cove, the French Provincial building first accommodated gold-seeking guests en route from Yerba Buena (San Francisco) to the Presidio. The Wamsley Art Center now houses art workshops and four suites complete with color TV, radio, full kitchen (one with a "coffee bar" only), and, of course, original artwork. The private accommodations off a garden and a sunny patio include two with fireplaces, and all have two entrances. Breakfast is self-serve in your own kitchen with eggs, croissants, cereals, juice, and coffee, tea or hot chocolate provided. A coffee maker also is furnished, along with easels for the artist-guest on the sunny deck. The inn is conveniently located in the marina area between the bay and Union Street.

The Bed and Breakfast Inn

4 Charlton Court, San Francisco, CA 94123
Phone: (415) 921-9784
Key: Inn; 10 units; Moderate-Del.; Limited smoking; No children under 7; No credit cards

This ten-room inn, located in a quiet nook near Union Street, is filled with family antiques and fresh flowers and offers garden views. A recent addition above the main house is a private suite with living room, kitchen, latticed balcony, and a spiral staircase leading to a loft bedroom.

Bock's Bed and Breakfast

1448 Willard Street, San Francisco, CA 94117
Phone: (415) 664-6842
Key: Home; 2 units; Inexpensive; No smoking; Children OK; No credit cards

This lovely Edwardian home in a residential section of the city is two blocks from Golden Gate Park and the University of California Medical Center. Guests may choose from either single or double accommodations with private bath, private entrance, refrigerator, in-room coffee and tea, TV, and telephone. Guests also have access to a washer and dryer; a deck is available. A continental breakfast is served in a dining room with original redwood paneling and magnificent views of the city. A two-night minimum stay is required; weekly rates are available.

Casa Arguello

225 Arguello Boulevard, San Francisco, CA 94118
Phone: (415) 752-9482
Key: Inn; 5 units; Inexpensive-Mod.; No smoking; No children under 8; No credit cards

Located in a residential area just ten minutes from the center of the city, this inn offers simple yet comfortable accommodations. A mixture of decor can be found throughout the spacious b&b, with an emphasis on the old. The complimentary breakfast is served in the dining room.

Edward II Inn

3155 Scott Street, San Francisco, CA 94123
Phone: (415) 922-3000
Key: Inn/Hotel; 33 units; Inexpensive-Del.; Smoking OK; Children OK; Credit cards

Located in the marina district, this 1915-vintage hotel offers close proximity to the shopping areas of Chestnut and Union streets. Recently redecorated throughout in an English country mood, the inn offers accommodations from the quaint to the deluxe. Four luxurious suites, two in the hotel and two in a nearby carriage house, are now offered and boast such amenities as canopy beds, wet bars, whirlpool baths, and more. The continental breakfast, hosted in the lobby area, is served by an Italian-French bakery located on the premises. An adjoining restaurant featuring Italian cuisine has recently been added. Parking is available in the surrounding neighborhood.

Fay Mansion Inn

834 Grove Street, San Francisco, CA 94117
Phone: (415) 921-1816
Key: Inn; 5 units; Moderate-Del.; Smoking OK; No children; No credit cards

161

This 1874 Italianate–Victorian house has been carefully restored and retains many of its original fixtures, including gas chandeliers, marble fireplaces, and a rare hand-painted–stenciled ceiling. A mixture of decor graces the guest rooms, all named after famous opera stars in honor of its last owner, Maude Fay. Guests enjoy a patio, hot tub, and garden.

Dorothy Franzblau

2331 Ninth Avenue, San Francisco, CA 94116
Phone: (415) 564-7686
Key: Home; 1 unit; Inexpensive; No smoking; Children OK; No credit cards

This home b&b offers a private suite with sitting room and bath. The comfortable stay includes a large breakfast and late-day snack. Guests enjoy ample street parking.

Hermitage House

2224 Sacramento Street, San Francisco, CA 94115
Phone: (415) 921-5515
Key: Inn; 5 units; Moderate-Exp.; Limited smoking; No children under 13; Credit cards

The historic redwood inn, just minutes from Nob Hill and downtown, offers both resident and overnight lodging. All rooms are furnished in antiques; many contain fireplaces, claw-foot tubs in the bath, and sitting areas. Guests enjoy a sun deck, a brick garden/courtyard, and spacious public rooms. There is a complimentary wine tasting each evening, and the breakfast fare includes fruit, cereal, breads, and a tray of meats and cheeses served by the fireplace.

Inn on Castro

321 Castro Street, San Francisco, CA 94114
Phone: (415) 861-0321

Key: Inn; 5 units; Moderate; Limited smoking; Children OK; Credit cards

This Victorian b&b offers a surprise of contemporary furnishings splashed with bright colors, vibrant paintings and an abundance of exotic plants and fresh flowers. Guests are served a breakfast of orange juice and fine pastries in the upstairs innkeeper's quarters, equally decorated in a contemporary yet hospitable motif. The inn is located on a hill with views of the city and bay.

The Inn San Francisco

943 South Van Ness Avenue, San Francisco, CA 94110
Phone: (415) 641-0188
Key: Inn; 15 units; Inexpensive-Del.; Smoking OK; No children under 12; Credit cards

This twenty-seven-room, 1872 Victorian mansion has been restored to its original grandeur and features cozy, spacious rooms. All guest rooms are furnished in antiques and boast fresh flowers, telephones, refrigerators, and televisions; several rooms offer private Jacuzzi tubs. The flower-filled garden with gazebo and hot tub, as well as the roof-top sun deck with panoramic city views, provides a pleasant retreat for guests. Each morning a deluxe, continental buffet breakfast is served in the double parlors.

The Inn at Union Square

440 Post Street, San Francisco, CA 94102
Phone: (415) 397-3510
Key: Inn/Hotel; 30 units; Expensive-Del.; Smoking OK; Children OK; Credit cards

Each guest room has been decorated with Georgian furnishings and colorful fabrics; most have king-size beds and sitting areas. Each floor hosts its own intimate lobby with a fireplace; these relaxing areas provide the sites for the morning breakfast of juice, fresh fruit, croissants, muffins, and scones and the afternoon tea with cakes and cucumber sandwiches. A sixth-floor suite has a fireplace, bar, whirlpool bath, and sauna. Other extras at the inn include terry robes in the room and the *Wall Street Journal* and *San Francisco Chronicle* outside each door in the morning.

The Mansion Hotel, San Francisco

The Mansion Hotel

2220 Sacramento Street, San Francisco, CA 94115
Phone: (415) 929-9444
Key: Inn/Hotel; 19 units; Expensive-Del.; Smoking OK; Children OK; Credit cards

Intimate parlor concerts, sculpture gardens, and a billiard room are unique offerings at this Queen Anne inn, located in a fine residential area. Many rooms boast marble fireplaces or private terraces; all are decorated in Victorian motif. A gourmet dinner is offered to guests only, and the complimentary breakfast of eggs, croissants, and juice is served in bed or in the breakfast kitchen.

Marina Inn B&B

3110 Octavia Street, San Francisco, CA 94123
Phone: (415) 928-1000
Key: Inn/Hotel; 40 units; Inexpensive-Mod.; Smoking OK; Children OK; Credit cards

This four-story Victorian hotel on the corner of Octavia and Lombard streets welcomes guests with its elegant marble lobby in country furnishings. The extensively renovated and redecorated inn with bay windows offers a second-floor sitting room, which is the locale of the morning continental breakfast and afternoon sherry; a microwave is provided here as well. Each of the forty rooms boast pastel-flowered wallpaper, forest green carpet, quilts, and full baths with marble sinks. Guest baskets, televisions, and telephones are also available in each guest room.

Millefiori Inn

444 Columbus Avenue, San Francisco, CA 94133
Phone: (415) 433-9111
Key: Inn/Hotel; 14 units; Moderate; Smoking OK; No children under 12; Credit cards

This continental-style hotel is located in the heart of North Beach. Stained-glass windows, brasswork, chandeliers, hardwood furniture, and European bath fixtures decorate throughout. Rooms have individual flower themes and boast private baths. A patio courtyard is the setting for a continental breakfast.

Moffatt House

431 Hugo Street, San Francisco, CA 94122
Phone: (415) 753-9279
Key: Inn; 4 units; Inexpensive; Smoking OK; Children OK; Credit cards

The 1910 Edwardian house near Golden Gate Park and the University of California Medical Center offers a casual, friendly

165

retreat with its light interiors, stained-glass windows, and flowering plants. Guests gather in the cheery kitchen for tourist information and a self-catered, generous continental breakfast of neighborhood-produce-market fruit, juice, home-baked muffins, toast, Danish, cheeses, and boiled eggs. The four guest rooms each accommodate up to four people and share baths. Queen-size, twin, and double beds are offered, and a crib is available for a one-time, nominal charge at this reasonable b&b.

The Monte Cristo

600 Presidio Avenue, San Francisco, CA 94115
Phone: (415) 931-1875 / 626-8777
Key: Inn/Hotel; 16 units; Moderate-Del.; Smoking OK; Children OK; Credit cards

The 1875-vintage inn is located just two blocks from restored Victorian shops. The spacious rooms are pleasantly furnished in authentic period pieces of Early American and English antiques, wallpapers, down comforters, and fragrant potpourri. A popular guest accommodation is the "Oriental Room" with Chinese wedding bed and sunken tub. The home-baked breakfast includes fresh juice, muffins, and cereals.

Pensione San Francisco

1668 Market Street, San Francisco, CA 94102
Phone: (415) 864-1271
Key: Inn/Hotel; 36 units; Inexpensive; Smoking OK; Children OK; Credit cards

Situated among antique shops, the inn is within walking distance of the Civic Center. The uniquely decorated guest rooms feature antique, western, and San Francisco motifs. All rooms feature their own vanity area with sink. Each floor of the hotel hosts a private guest lounge.

Petite Auberge

863 Bush Street, San Francisco, CA 94108
Phone: (415) 928-6000
Key: Inn/Hotel; 26 units; Expensive-Del.; Limited smoking; Children OK; Credit cards

This romantic French country inn in the heart of downtown is a finely restored mansion offering an ornate, Baroque exterior design and warm, burnished woods on the interior. An antique carousel horse and fresh flowers greet guests, and an antique-filled lounge with fireplace is a cozy retreat. The twenty-six guest rooms all feature private baths, French wallpapers, antiques, handmade pillows, and quilted bedspreads; eighteen rooms boast fireplaces. A garden-view dining area offers a generous continental fare each morning, as well as afternoon tea. Among the special services extended to the pampered guests at the b&b is expert shoe polishing by inn "elves" each night.

The Queen Anne

1590 Sutter Street, San Francisco, CA 94109
Phone: (415) 441-2828 / (800) 262-2663
Key: Inn/Hotel; 49 units; Expensive-Del.; Smoking OK; Children OK; Credit cards

In the heart of the Civic Center area, this nineteenth-century refurbished guest house is a classic Queen Anne example with a cascading staircase, glass skylights, and window settees. Room furnishings blend the old and new with marble sinks, brick fireplaces, and antiques. The continental breakfast, along with the morning newspaper, is served in the room; afternoon tea and sherry are offered in the parlor. Laundry and business arrangements are available.

The Red Victorian

1665 Haight Street, San Francisco, CA 94117
Phone: (415) 864-1978 / 864-1906

Key: Inn/Hotel; 15 units; Inexpensive-Del.; No smoking; Children OK; Credit cards

This small upstairs hotel is as colorful as the well-known Haight-Ashbury neighborhood in which it resides. Teddy bears, red rugs, and lace curtains grace the inn and its uniquely decorated shared- and private-bath guest accommodations. A continental breakfast of croissants, muffins, and coffee is served in the bay-windowed "pink parlor." The bed & breakfast accommodations are a part of an entire complex that includes an art gallery, a human-relationship center, and a staff-training program.

Riley's Bed & Breakfast

1324 6th Avenue, San Francisco, CA 94122
Phone: (415) 731-0788
Key: Home; 3 units; Inexpensive; Smoking OK; Children OK; Credit cards

This budget-minded b&b is located conveniently between Golden Gate Park and the University of California Medical Center. The 1908 Victorian home is furnished in antiques and offers three guest rooms which share baths. Bakery croissants, orange juice, and freshly ground coffee or tea are included in the stay here and are served in the old-fashioned, sunny kitchen.

The Spreckels Mansion

737 Buena Vista West, San Francisco, CA 94117
Phone: (415) 861-3008
Key: Inn; 11 units; Moderate-Del.; Limited smoking; No children; Credit cards

Built in 1887, this grand family home has a rich history. Located on a hilltop overlooking the city, with plentiful parking, the inn is decorated in authentic Victorian-period furnishings yet offers modern conveniences such as direct-line phones. Decor highlights include a freestanding tub that fronts a fireplace, large sitting areas, and a penthouse suite with a bar/kitchen, skylights, and stained glass. The continental breakfast is served in-room.

Stanyan Park Hotel

750 Stanyan Street, San Francisco, CA 94117
Phone: (415) 751-1000
Key: Inn/Hotel; 36 units; Moderate; Smoking OK; Children OK;
Credit cards

This hotel of the early 1900s has been meticulously restored
to its early glory, including the reconstruction of its rare cupola
and roof balustrade. The thirty-six guest rooms and suites are
individually decorated in Victorian furnishings, four-poster beds,
brass chandeliers, and patterned wallpapers and have the modern
amenities of phones, color TV, and private tiled bathrooms with
pedestal sinks. Many of the guest accommodations overlook
Golden Gate Park, and guests may park across the street from the
b&b in an attended lot. Coffee, juice, croissants, and sweet rolls
are served in the hotel dining room each morning.

Union Street Inn

2229 Union Street, San Francisco, CA 94123
Phone: (415) 346-0424
Key: Inn/Cottage; 6 units; Moderate-Del.; Limited smoking; No
children; Credit cards

The nineteenth-century Edwardian home-turned-inn has a
garden setting within the city's downtown. The European-style
decor includes canopy and brass beds, armoires, and sinks in each
room. A carriage house is separated from the inn by a garden and
Jacuzzi, which are enjoyed by guests. The continental breakfast is
served in the parlor, the garden, or the room.

Victorian Inn on the Park

301 Lyon Street, San Francisco, CA 94117
Phone: (415) 931-1830
Key: Inn; 12 units; Moderate-Del.; Smoking OK; No children un-
der 5; Credit cards

Near Golden Gate Park in an area famed for its Victorian
architecture, the 1897 inn also reflects turn-of-the-century San

169

Francisco in its furnishings. Each room offers fresh flowers, comforters, down pillows, and private bath; some guest rooms boast fireplaces. Along with fruit and home-baked croissants comes a daily newspaper in the oak-paneled dining room each morning. Phones and television are available on request; the inn is able to accommodate small meetings.

The Washington Square Inn

1660 Stockton Street, San Francisco, CA 94133
Phone: (415) 981-4220
Key: Inn/Hotel; 15 units; Moderate-Del.; Smoking OK; Children OK; Credit cards

The small hotel is located in the heart of the city's Italian district on historic Washington Square. Most guest rooms, decorated individually in English and French antiques, boast private baths, and all have telephones. A complimentary breakfast of croissants, fresh juice, and coffee is served in bed or by the hearth.

The White Swan Inn

845 Bush Street, San Francisco, CA 94108
Phone: (415) 775-1755
Key: Inn/Hotel; 27 units; Expensive-Del.; Limited smoking; Children OK; Credit cards

This recently renovated b&b is filled with English country charm created by the use of rich, warm woods, soft wallpapers, and an abundance of cozy fireplaces. The uniquely decorated guest rooms and two-room suite feature fireplaces, refrigerators, private baths, telephones, and color TV as well as bay windows, fresh flowers and fruit, antiques, and overstuffed chairs. Guests will enjoy the generous breakfast in the dining room or in the solarium off the courtyard-sheltered garden. An English high tea is served each afternoon in the peaceful English garden; a fireside living room and library offer restful retreats as well. Innkeepers at this downtown b&b pamper guests by making sure guests' shoes are polished, their guest-room fire is kindled, and the morning newspaper waits outside each door.

The Willows

710 14th Street, San Francisco, CA 94114
Phone: (415) 431-4770
Key: Inn/Hotel; 11 units; Moderate; Smoking OK; No children under 11; Credit cards

Convenient to downtown and Union Square, the inn also provides parking for guests. Rooms are individually furnished in "gypsy willow" furniture designed for the inn, antiques, armoires (with robes), Laura Ashley prints, and private phones. The continental breakfast, served in bed or in the sitting room, arrives with a morning paper. The "Hour of Aperitif" each afternoon offers chilled wine to guests. The inn gives priority reservations to guests at its small French restaurant.

Burlingame Bed & Breakfast

1021 Balboa Avenue, Burlingame, CA 94010
Phone: (415) 344-5815
Key: Home; 1 unit; Inexpensive; No smoking; Children OK; No credit cards

This quiet two-story home surrounded by oak trees and redwoods is just three miles south of the airport. The innkeepers at this home b&b are happy to pick up guests at, or deliver them to, the airport. The upstairs guest room offers views of the creek and gardens, a king-size bed, and private bath; a rollaway bed is available for a fourth person. Guests enjoy a color TV, a picnic area, and a separate area where the morning breakfast of juice, fruit, and croissants is served on fine china. The innkeeper speaks Spanish and has knowledge of several other languages.

Gramma's Inn

2740 Telegraph Avenue, Berkeley, CA 94705
Phone: (415) 549-2145
Key: Inn; 29 units; Moderate-Del.; Limited smoking; No children under 7; Credit cards

Gramma's Inn, Berkeley

Two side-by-side, turn-of-the-century homes with gardens, a carriage house, and garden house form this recently expanded b&b not far from the university campus. The Queen Anne original b&b structure offers two parlors, a fireplace, ornate moldings, inlaid floors, and chintz fabrics and antiques. The adjacent Fay House has marble fireplaces, hand-painted ceilings, stained-glass windows, and oriental rugs. The unique guest accommodations with private baths (except for two rooms) offer such amenities as antiques, fireplaces, private decks, armoires, and stained-glass windows. The breakfast of croissants, muffins, fruit platters, Gramma's granola, and juice is served in the dining room, the garden, or the greenhouse. The inn is a favorite locale for weddings and serves a gourmet Sunday brunch.

Captain Dillingham's Inn

145 East "D" Street, Benicia, CA 94510
Phone: (707) 746-7164 / (800) 544-2278
Key: Inn; 10 units; Moderate-Exp.; Smoking OK; Children OK; Credit cards

This former 1853-built home of a seafaring captain is located in the town's historic waterfront district, just one-half block from the marina. The restored, yellow, Cape Cod–style home is surrounded by lush gardens and offers spacious guest rooms, including one suite. Guest accommodations all feature private baths with Jacuzzi tubs (except for the "Mate's Quarters" with its claw-foot tub), antique decor, and modern amenities such as television, radio, refrigerators, telephones, and air conditioning. The "Captain's Quarters" features a working onyx fireplace; several rooms offer garden-view decks. The buffet breakfast, served in the country dining room or on one of the outside decks, includes fresh fruits, breads, pastries, cheeses, meats, cereals, yogurts, juices, and the inn's special blend of coffee. Wine-and-cheese trays are brought to the rooms each afternoon.

The Union Hotel

401 First Street, Benicia, CA 94510
Phone: (707) 746-0100
Key: Inn/Hotel; 12 units; Moderate-Exp.; Smoking OK; Children OK; Credit cards

This 1882 hotel with spectacular views of the bay has been completely restored with modern conveniences such as sound-proofing, an elevator, phones, television, and private baths with Jacuzzi tubs. Each one of the guest rooms reflects a less-than-modern era ranging from late-1800s Americana through nineteenth-century Louis XVI to 1920s art deco. A restaurant on the premises specializes in French cuisine and serves the continental breakfast, which is included in the stay. The inn is located two blocks from the new marina.

The Victorian on Lytton

555 Lytton Avenue, Palo Alto, CA 94301
Phone: (415) 322-8555
Key: Inn; 10 units; Moderate-Del.; No smoking; No children under 15; Credit cards

This historic inn, built in 1895 as a private residence, also provides accommodations in a newly constructed addition in the rear; the grounds are graced by a fragrant, English country garden. The ten unique guest rooms are named after Queen Victoria and her nine children and offer such "royal" touches as separate sit-

The Victorian on Lytton, Palo Alto

ting parlors, private baths, canopy or four-poster queen- or king-size beds, romantic laces, and fine antiques. The "Queen's Room" features a unique step-down bathroom. A generous continental breakfast is served in the room between 7:00 A.M. and 9:00 A.M. along with the morning paper; complimentary port and sherry with cheeses is served each evening. Guests may relax in the tastefully decorated parlor with classical music; coffee, tea, and biscuits are available throughout the day. The service-minded hosts at this b&b near Stanford University will often offer special courtesies such as laundry and ironing when their guests need assistance.

The Madison Street Inn

1390 Madison Street, Santa Clara, CA 95050
Phone: (408) 249-5541/249-6058
Key: Inn; 5 units; Moderate; Limited smoking; No children under 5; Credit cards

This restored Queen Anne home in grays and blues is located in a quiet residential area and has a pretty yard with red-brick pool, redwood deck, and hot tub. Guests enjoy a parlor decorated in oriental rugs and comfortable antiques, and its fireplace. The five antique-filled guest rooms with high ceilings are wallpapered and have plush peach carpeting. Three of the guest rooms have private baths, and the two rooms that share a bath have sink/ vanity areas. Breakfast treats at the inn may include Belgian waffles, eggs Benedict, and fresh blueberry muffins; the repast may be enjoyed in your room, on the patio, or in the dining room. A television, VCR, and movies are available, as are bicycles. Complimentary sherry is offered at all times, and dinner is provided on arrangement. The inn offers package stays for room, dinner, and tickets to the Winchester Mystery House.

Montara B&B

P.O. Box 493, 1125 Tamarind Street, Montara, CA 94037
Phone: (415) 728-3946
Key: Home; 1 unit; Inexpensive; No smoking; No children; No credit cards

This home b&b, nestled in a quiet coastal town just twenty-five minutes from downtown San Francisco, offers guests a myriad of surrounding activities, such as beach going, whale watching, horseback riding, and hiking. The redwood-and-glass contemporary home offers a sunny solarium overlooking a colorful garden, which is the locale of the full morning breakfast featuring the inn's own honey. The one guest accommodation is a suite with private bath and entrance; a redwood sunning deck; a private, connecting sitting room, where evening sherry and nuts are provided; and either a queen-size bed or twin beds made from a trundle. The suite offers comfortable furnishings and tall, airy windows; television is available on request.

The Pillar Point Inn

P.O. Box 388, El Granada, CA 94018
380 Capistrano Road, Princeton-By-the-Sea, CA 94018
Phone: (415) 728-7377
Key: Inn; 11 units; Expensive-Del.; Limited smoking; No children under 12; Credit cards

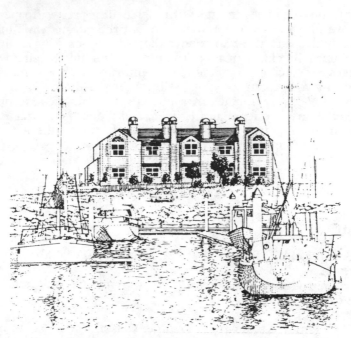

The Pillar Point Inn, El Granada

Located on the only harbor between San Francisco and Santa Cruz is this newly constructed, Cape Cod–style b&b that proves a haven for homesick New Englanders. The new inn was built to blend with the architecture of the quaint fishing village and offers eleven luxurious guest accommodations, all with views of the harbor, Half Moon Bay, and the Pacific Ocean. Each room offers a fireplace, private bath, European-style feather mattress, and bay or window seat, as well as VCR, concealed television, radio, and refrigerator. Five of the rooms boast a private steam bath. A public dining room and living room share an open fireplace and are furnished in country pine and maple; a separate conference room accommodates up to twenty persons. The complimentary morning fare served in the room or in the dining room, includes eggs, meat, bread, and fruit dishes; champagne is available on request. A harbor-view terrace is the site of afternoon tea or wine.

Old Thyme Inn

779 Main Street, Half Moon Bay, CA 94019
Phone: (415) 726-1616
Key: Inn; 6 units; Inexpensive-Exp.; Limited smoking; Children OK mid-week only; No credit cards

Located in Main Street's historic district, this 1899-built b&b is within walking distance to quaint boutiques and restaurants. In the rear of the redwood-constructed Victorian is an herb garden with more than fifty varieties of sweet-smelling herbs. Guests may explore the garden, which provides garnishes and breakfast ingredients. The many return guests to this new b&b may choose from six individual accommodations ranging from the cozy "Chamomile Room," with shared bath and antique American decor, to the plush "Thyme Room," with double-size whirlpool tub in the private bathroom, a fireplace and a queen-size canopy bed. Four of the guest rooms feature private baths. The "English-style" morning fare typically includes such specialties as fresh juice, coffee, homemade scones, cold meats, and English cheeses as well as homemade French cherry flan; the menu varies each morning. Both breakfast and evening wine and sherry are served in the lounge by a cozy fire.

San Benito House

356 Main Street, Half Moon Bay, CA 94019
Phone: (415) 726-3425
Key: Inn/Hotel; 12 units; Inexpensive-Exp.; Smoking OK; Children on approval; Credit cards

This upstairs historic hostelry is filled with European antiques and fresh flowers from the English garden. Guest rooms bordering the garden boast more elaborate decor. The continental breakfast is served in the room or on the sunny redwood deck, which is dressed with flower boxes and a massive firepit for the evening cognac. A "nonhistoric" sauna is available as well as lunch and dinner in the hotel's Garden Deli and San Benito House Restaurant.

New Davenport Bed & Breakfast

31 Davenport Avenue, Davenport, CA 95017
Phone: (408) 425-1818 / 426-4122
Key: Inn; 12 units; Moderate-Exp.; No smoking; No children under 13; Credit cards

Housed in one of the town's original old buildings, the inn is within walking distance of local craft studios and close to a popular whale-watch spot. The guest rooms, all with private bath, are furnished with antique iron beds, oak dressers, colorful rugs, and art and are located above the restaurant with ocean views or in an adjacent house with patio and sitting room. Champagne is offered on arrival, and the continental breakfast featuring home-baked cinnamon rolls is served in the Cash Store Restaurant next door.

CENTRAL CALIFORNIA

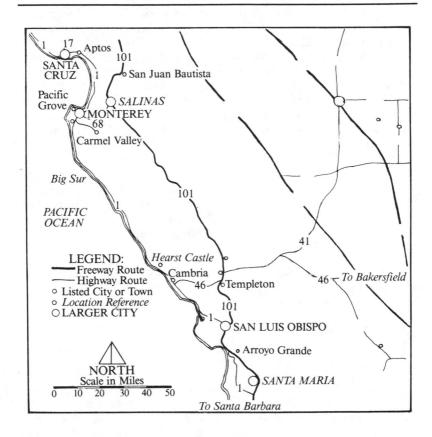

CENTRAL COAST

California's Central Coast offers an array of small communities that dot the dramatic Pacific coast with unparalleled "Mediterranean" sunbathing beaches plus rich historical offerings. Original California missions can be found in several towns, such as San Juan Bautista, San Miguel, Carmel, and San Luis Obispo, and along with them stately examples of turn-of-the-century architecture, tree-lined streets, and coastal beauty. This region may be best known for the Hearst Castle in San Simeon, the state's most popular tourist attraction after Disneyland. But this region is becoming known for its grape-growing industry, as wineries and vineyards are beginning to compete with wine country as the state's "Little Napa." Travelers may stroll the boardwalk in Santa Cruz, observe the butterfly migration in Pacific Grove, and enjoy the quaint shops of Carmel, the "living Mission" and annual Mozart Festival in San Luis Obispo, and the unending, peaceful country drives through the rolling hills and wildflowers of the inland valleys.

Chateau Des Fleurs

7995 Highway 9, Ben Lomond, CA 95005
Phone: (408) 336-8943
Key: Inn; 3 units; Moderate-Exp.; No smoking; No children under 16; Credit cards

This late-1870s Victorian mansion was once owned by the Bartlett family of pear fame; its pear trees still bear fruit for the morning breakfast. Guests may lounge on the front deck or wander through the garden with wishing well, flowers, fruit trees, and vegetables. The three spacious guest rooms, decorated in floral themes, feature private baths, iron and brass queen-size beds, ornate ceiling fans, and down comforters; the "Rose Room" boasts an in-room claw-foot tub on a raised platform. The "Gallery" common room with cozy, antique woodstove contains a library, stereo, television, piano, and organ. Breakfast, served in the formal dining room, includes homemade cinnamon rolls, muffins, coffee cake, fresh fruit, and a main course such as quiche, cheese blintzes, soufflés, omelettes, or Belgian waffles; French-blend coffee and juices are offered in the Gallery before breakfast. Guests enjoy sparkling cider, eggnogs, and cheese and crackers between 6:00 P.M. and 7:00 P.M.

The Babbling Brook Bed & Breakfast Inn

1025 Laurel Street, Santa Cruz, CA 95060
Phone: (408) 427-2437
Key: Inn; 12 units; Moderate-Exp.; Smoking OK; Children (under 12) on approval; Credit cards

Cascading waterfalls, a meandering creek, and an acre of gardens, pines, and redwoods surround this secluded inn built on the foundation of a 1790s tannery and an Ohlone Indian village. The dozen guest accommodations offer country French decor, private baths, telephones, television, fireplaces, private decks, and outside entrances; two rooms feature Jacuzzi bathtubs. A country breakfast and afternoon wine are included in the stay. The inn is within walking distance of the beach, wharf, shopping, and tennis.

Chateau Victorian

118 First Street, Santa Cruz, CA 95060
Phone: (408) 458-9458
Key: Inn; 7 units; Moderate-Exp.; No smoking; No children; Credit cards

This turn-of-the-century inn was originally a single family home and also an apartment complex in the 1950s. Just one block from the boardwalk and beach, all guest rooms offer queen-size beds and private tiled baths as well as fireplaces. A continental breakfast of fruit, juice, and croissants is served in the lounge dining room, on the deck, or on the rooftop terrace.

Cliff Crest

407 Cliff Street, Santa Cruz, CA 95060
Phone: (408) 427-2609
Key: Inn; 5 units; Moderate-Exp.; No smoking; Children on approval; Credit cards

This 1887 estate is a historical landmark noted for its gardens and close proximity to the ocean. Each guest room has its own

181

bath, antique furnishings, and fresh flowers; many offer views of the Pacific. The smallest unit, the "Pineapple Room," boasts a pineapple-carved four-poster bed and an 1887 stained-glass window, and the "Empire Room" offers a king-size four-poster bed and fireplace. The full breakfast features juice, fresh fruit, muffins or coffee cake, and a main entree such as quiche or a frittata and is served in the room or in the downstairs solarium.

The Darling House, Santa Cruz

The Darling House

314 West Cliff Drive, Santa Cruz, CA 95060
Phone: (408) 458-1958
Key: Inn/Cottage; 8 units; Moderate-Del.; Limited smoking; Children OK (cottage only); Credit cards

The sweeping verandas of this preserved Mission Revival home that was built in 1910 overlook the Pacific Ocean and Monterey Bay. The ocean-side grounds of the residence are filled with citrus trees, roses, palms, and blossoms. The interior of the house has eight different inlaid hardwoods found on walls, floors, and doors as well as beveled glass, stenciled borders, and open-hearth fireplaces. The guest rooms and separate cottage are decorated in period pieces with Tiffany lamps, matching antique bedroom suites, and cozy down comforters and pillows. The cottage sleeps a family of four. Breakfast consists of goodies made from scratch and is served in the ocean-view dining room. Guests enjoy evening wine and champagne that carry the inn's own label, and innkeepers can arrange horse-drawn carriage rides along the ocean.

Apple Lane Inn

6265 Soquel Drive, Aptos, CA 95003
Phone: (408) 475-6868
Key: Inn; 5 units; Moderate; Limited smoking; No children; Credit cards

This restored Victorian farmhouse was built in the 1870s among apple orchards and vineyards. Before walking to the nearby beach or visiting the local wineries, guests are invited to partake of a game of darts in the Cider Room. The five antique-decorated guest rooms offer both private and shared baths. The farmhouse inn, set in two and one-half acres of gardens, vineyards, and fields, serves a full country breakfast.

Mangels House

P.O. Box 302, 570 Aptos Creek Road, Aptos, CA 95001
Phone: (408) 688-7982
Key: Inn; 5 units; Moderate-Exp.; Limited smoking; No children under 13; Credit cards

This country Victorian house built in the 1880s is situated on four acres of garden and lawn and overlooks the State Redwood Forest, just two-thirds of a mile from the beach. The spacious rooms with high ceilings are decorated in a combination of antiques and painted pieces. A sitting room with library and piano is the locale of evening Dubonnet, cheese, and crackers by the large stone fireplace. The guest rooms, offering both shared and private baths, contain wash basins and individual touches such as wallpaper or stenciling and unusual art. The "Mauve Room" boasts its own marble fireplace. A full breakfast featuring fresh herb omelettes is included in the stay; guests may use the inn refrigerator for storing wine and picnic foods.

183

Bed & Breakfast San Juan

P.O. Box 613, 315 the Alameda, San Juan Bautista, CA 95045
Phone: (408) 623-4101
Key: Home; 5 units; Moderate; Smoking OK; Children OK; No credit cards

The 1858 Wilcox-Lang House, a well-established b&b home, is just two blocks from historic downtown San Juan Bautista. Guests here may stroll to the mission with its graceful arches, to California's second-most-visited State Historic Park, and to various boutiques and restaurants. The five guest rooms and the common room at the b&b feature period American furnishings; reservations are required in advanced.

Centrella Hotel, Pacific Grove

Centrella Hotel

612 Central Avenue, P.O. Box 51157, Pacific Grove, CA 93950
Phone: (408) 372-3372
Key: Inn/Hotel/Cottages; 27 units; Moderate-Del.; Limited smoking; Children OK; Credit cards

Located at the tip of the Monterey Peninsula, this century-old Victorian hotel invites guests to enjoy its brick walkways and surrounding gardens. The morning paper is delivered to each room, attic suite, and cottage. All accommodations are appointed with hand-selected antiques and private baths with claw-foot tubs. All suites feature skylights, wet bars, and color TV, while cottages contain fireplaces, TV, refrigerators, and wet bars. Both the complimentary breakfast and evening wine and hors d'oeuvres are served buffet style before a cheery fire.

The Gosby House

643 Lighthouse Avenue, Pacific Grove, CA 93950
Phone: (408) 375-1287
Key: Inn; 23 units; Moderate-Exp.; Limited smoking; Children OK (some rooms); Credit cards

In the heart of historic Pacific Grove, this tastefully restored Queen Anne mansion with rounded corner tower and bay windows offers two parlors, one offering late-afternoon tea by the fire and one that hosts the generous buffet breakfast, which may be taken to the garden or to the room on a tray. The guest rooms feature polished natural woods, comforters, delicate wallpaper prints, ruffled curtains, armoires, fireplaces, and fresh fruit, and all but two accommodations have private baths with antique claw-foot tubs or showers. Two suites offer kitchenettes. Hot cider, sherry, or tea are offered each evening.

Green Gables Inn

104 Fifth Street, Pacific Grove, CA 93950
Phone: (408) 375-2095
Key: Inn; 11 units; Expensive-Del.; Limited smoking; Children OK (some rooms); Credit cards

This half-timbered, step-gabled mansion on the edge of the Pacific Grove shoreline offers a panoramic view of Monterey Bay. The living room, with bay-window seating, antiques, and stained-glass–adorned fireplace, is the locale of afternoon tea. Each morning a generous breakfast is served in the dining room or in the cozy living-room alcoves. The guest accommodations include upstairs rooms and guest rooms in the carriage house across the courtyard. Rooms feature soft colors, views, flowers, fruit, cozy quilts, and antiques. Suites at the inn have sitting rooms or areas with fireplaces, bedrooms, and private baths.

The House of Seven Gables Inn, Pacific Grove

The House of Seven Gables Inn

555 Ocean View Boulevard, Pacific Grove, CA 93950
Phone: (408) 372-4341
Key: Inn; 14 units; Moderate-Del.; No smoking; No children under 12; No credit cards

Spectacular ocean views are enjoyed from each of the fourteen guest rooms at this 1886-built Victorian inn. Each guest room boasts a private bath, elegant European antiques, oriental rugs, chandeliers, and antique stained-glass windows. A generous continental breakfast is served in the stately dining room with chandelier; high tea is offered each day at 4:00 P.M. The inn is conveniently located near all of the Monterey Peninsula attractions.

Roserox Country Inn By-The-Sea

557 Ocean View Boulevard, Pacific Grove, CA 93950
Phone: (408) 373-7673
Key: Inn; 8 units; Expensive-Del.; Limited smoking; No children under 12; No credit cards

This four-story, turn-of-the-century inn on the ocean has retained its original hardwood floors and ten-foot-high ceilings with redwood beams. The guest rooms are furnished with antique beds that range from brass with mother-of-pearl inlays to a 110-year-old American oak bed. All of the accommodations share claw-foot–tub baths with ocean views and are outfitted with designer linens, imported soaps, down comforters, and a special "gift" to remind guests of their stay at Roserox. The generous buffet featuring freshly ground Cartagena coffee can be served in bed, on one of the ocean-view patios, or in the "Morning Room." Guests gather around the parlor fireplace in the evening for complimentary wine, beer, soft drinks, and hors d'oeuvres.

The Jabberwock

598 Laine Street, Monterey, CA 93940
Phone: (408) 372-4777
Key: Inn; 7 units; Moderate-Del.; No smoking; No children under 15; No credit cards

Goose-down pillows, huge Victorian beds, lace sheets, and fresh flowers await guests who visit this converted convent that is only four blocks from Cannery Row and the Monterey Bay Aquarium and near the seventeen-mile drive. Guests enjoy the living-room sun porch that overlooks fern falls or the estate gardens, the site of evening hors d'oeuvres and apéritifs. The breakfasts, which are "razzleberry flabjous," are served fireside in the elegant dining room or in the room; the innkeepers "tuck" guests into bed with cookies and milk. The guest rooms feature two garret suites on the third floor that share a secluded sitting room and views.

187

Old Monterey Inn, Monterey

Old Monterey Inn

500 Martin Street, Monterey, CA 93940
Phone: (408) 375-8284
Key: Inn/Cottage; 10 units; Deluxe; No smoking; No children; No credit cards

Surrounded by an acre of landscaped grounds with gardens and old oak trees, this 1920s English country home is within walking distance of the historic sites of Monterey. The living room tempts guests with a warming fireplace and a sampling of wines and cheeses. Rooms feature wicker and English antiques, skylights, fireplaces, and garden views. A separate cottage has stained glass and a bay-window seat. The full breakfast is served in the dining room or in the room.

The Spindrift Inn

P.O. Box 3196, 652 Cannery Row, Monterey, CA 93940
Phone: (408) 646-8900; (800) 841-1879
Key: Inn/Hotel; 42 units; Deluxe; Smoking OK; Children OK; Credit cards

Once referred to as the "old Chinese hotel" by author John Steinbeck, this hotel b&b has been totally rebuilt after years of being vacant. The tastefully appointed, four-story inn has a New

Orleans look and boasts colorful flower boxes. Its superb location is just one and one-half blocks from the new aquarium, directly on the beach in Cannery Row. All forty-two guest rooms are distinctly decorated and furnished with canopies, sleigh beds, imported fabrics, feather beds, oriental carpets, window seats, fireplaces, and comforters; some rooms have saunas. Guest rooms offer such extras as remote control TV in armoires, nightly turn-down service, refrigerators, and Swiss chocolates, and all rooms have private marble-and-brass baths with second telephone. The continental breakfast arrives with the morning newspaper on a silver tray and is enjoyed in the room. Afternoon tea is offered, and guests may relax on the roof garden with ocean vistas.

The Cobblestone Inn, Carmel

The Cobblestone Inn

P.O. Box 3185, Junipero between 7th & 8th, Carmel, CA 93921
Phone: (408) 625-5222; (800) AAA-INNS
Key: Inn/Hotel; 24 units; Moderate-Exp.; Limited smoking; Children OK; Credit cards

This country inn with an English country-garden atmosphere is just two blocks from the heart of Carmel's quaint shops and

189

cafés. Guests cross a cobblestone courtyard to enter the living room and lounge with large stone fireplace; it is here that guests gather for tea, sherry, wine, and hors d'oeuvres. The two dozen guest rooms feature country antiques, romantic fireplaces, private baths, fresh fruit and flowers, soft quilts, wall-to-wall carpeting, and color TV. Two suites are offered at the inn. A generous breakfast is served in the dining room or on the courtyard terrace, and picnic lunches may be ordered. As a special touch, the innkeepers will see that any shoes or golf clubs left outside a guest room door are polished by the time guests open the door for their morning paper.

Cypress Inn

P.O. Box Y, Carmel, CA 93921
Phone: (408) 624-3871
Key: Inn/Hotel; 33 units; Moderate-Del.; Smoking OK; Children OK (certain areas only); Credit cards

Originally opened in 1929, this landmark Spanish Mediterranean inn was carefully renovated in 1986. Located in the heart of Carmel Village, the inn features a spacious living room with fireplace and an intimate library overlooking a private garden/courtyard. A variety of rooms are offered to guests, most with oversized beds and all with private baths, telephones, and color cable televisions; some units boast sitting areas, wet bars, verandas, and ocean views. A continental breakfast is offered each morning.

Farmhouse Inn at Mission Ranch Resort

26270 Dolores, Carmel, CA 93923
Phone: (408) 624-6436
Key: Inn; 6 units; Inexpensive-Mod.; Smoking OK; No children; Credit cards

The 125-year-old farmhouse is just part of the twenty-acre Mission Ranch Resort, which also includes motel and cottage accommodations, a restaurant with piano bar, private party barn, and eight tennis courts. The inn features turn-of-the-century decor and serves a continental breakfast in the fireside parlor.

Happy Landing Inn

P.O. Box 2619, Monte Verde & 5th Streets, Carmel, CA 93921
Phone: (408) 624-7917
Key: Inn/Cottage; 7 units; Moderate-Exp.; Limited smoking; No children under 12; Credit cards

This 1925 Comstock-designed inn features guest rooms and a honeymoon cottage with antiques and cathedral ceilings. All rooms open onto a central garden with a pond and gazebo. Centrally located, the inn is just four blocks from the beach. The breakfast is served in the room each morning and features homemade breads and muffins, fresh fruit, and juice. A spacious lounge with cathedral ceilings and a stone fireplace offers daytime refreshments and relaxation.

Holiday House

P.O. Box 782, Camino Real at 7th Avenue, Carmel, CA 93921
Phone: (408) 624-6267
Key: Inn; 6 units; Moderate; No smoking; No children under 14; No credit cards

Built in 1905, this quiet, residential-area inn has been hosting guests for more than fifty years. The brown-shingled house on a hillside with colorful gardens, fountain, and fish ponds offers ocean views from the sun porch surrounded by pines. The individually decorated guest rooms offer such touches as slanted ceilings, ocean views, brass beds, and needlepoint, and four rooms have private baths. A spacious living room with stone fireplace is the spot to relax, sip sherry, or enjoy the morning breakfast, which includes juice, cereals, fruit, sweet rolls and muffins, egg dishes, and beverages.

San Antonio House

P.O. Box 3683, Carmel, CA 93921
Phone: (408) 624-4334

Key: Inn; 4 units; Moderate-Exp.; Smoking OK; No children under 12; No credit cards

All four guest rooms at the inn have their own entrance, telephone, refrigerator, television, and private bath plus lots of antiques and paintings. The two-story, turn-of-the-century house is surrounded by trees, gardens, lawns, and stone terraces.

Sandpiper Inn

2408 Bay View Avenue, Carmel, CA 93923
Phone: (408) 624-6433
Key: Inn; 15 units; Moderate-Exp.; Smoking OK; No children under 12; Credit cards

Offering a spectacular view of the ocean, the inn is within a pleasant walk of downtown. The guest rooms are decorated in antiques, and all have private baths. Breakfast is served at a large, formal dining-room table in the lounge, where television and the morning paper are also available. The inn offers bicycle rentals.

Sea View Inn

P.O. Box 4138, Carmel, CA 93921
Phone: (408) 624-8778
Key: Inn; 8 units; Moderate; No smoking; No children under 12; Credit cards

This 1906 three-story guest house is furnished with both antiques and contemporary pieces and has been redecorated throughout. Located just three blocks from the ocean and five blocks from town, it is situated centrally. Guest rooms, mostly with private bath, feature bay-window seats and large beds; one room features an intricate canopy bed with coordinated fabrics and wall covering. The homemade breakfast consists of fruit, juice, and muffins or coffee cake and is served fireside in the parlor, the site of afternoon sherry as well.

The Stonehouse Inn

8th below Monte Verde, P.O. Box 2517, Carmel, CA 93921
Phone: (408) 624-4569
Key: Inn; 8 units; Moderate-Exp.; No smoking; No children under 12; No credit cards

The turn-of-the-century home is most notable for its stone exterior, hand-shaped by Indians around 1906. The guest rooms, named after famous artist/guests from earlier days, feature airy colors, antiques, homemade quilts, and fresh fruit. The large continental breakfast is offered in the dining room or garden or by the large stone fireplace. Downtown is only two blocks away.

Sundial Lodge

P.O. Box J, Carmel, CA 93921
Phone: (408) 624-8578
Key: Inn/Hotel; 19 units; Moderate; Smoking OK; Children OK; Credit cards

This small hotel in the heart of town offers nineteen charming rooms decorated with wicker, French country, or Victorian furnishings. All guest rooms offer private baths, touch-tone telephones, and color television. Guests enter their rooms through the flower-filled courtyard; most accommodations boast ocean or garden views. The stay at Sundial includes a continental breakfast with homemade muffins and a relaxing afternoon tea.

Vagabond's House

P.O. Box 2747, Carmel, CA 93921
Phone: (408) 624-7738
Key: Inn; 11 units; Moderate-Exp.; Smoking OK; No children; Credit cards

This English Tudor country inn features wood-burning fireplaces and refrigerators or kitchens in each antique-decorated guest room. All rooms, some with "treetop" views, look out onto the flagstone courtyard filled with oaks, ferns, flowers, and assorted hanging plants. Each room has its own coffeepot, complete with fresh-ground coffee, and a decanter of sherry. A continental breakfast is served each morning in the room.

Robles Del Rio Lodge

200 Punta Del Monte, Carmel Valley, CA 93924
Phone: (408) 659-3705
Key: Inn/Cottages; 31 units; Moderate-Exp.; Smoking OK; Children OK; Credit cards

This 1920s lodge was built originally as a private club and claims to be the oldest lodge still operating in the valley. The rustic resort sits on a mountain top with panoramic views of sunny Carmel Valley. The thirty-one guest rooms and cottages range in decor from delicate Laura Ashley prints to board-and-batten country ambiance. Accommodations offer armoire-enclosed cable television; the cottages boast kitchenettes and fireplaces. A complimentary morning breakfast consisting of freshly baked muffins and breads, hard-boiled eggs, seasonal fruit, pastries, freshly squeezed juice, coffee, and herbal teas is served each morning around the large stone fireplace of the main-lodge living room. The Ridge Restaurant at the lodge serves French country–cuisine lunches and dinners to guests and the public everyday except Monday.

The Valley Lodge

P.O. Box 93, Carmel Valley & Ford Roads, Carmel, CA 93924
Phone: (408) 659-2261
Key: Inn/Cottages; 31 units; Moderate-Exp.; Smoking OK; Children OK; Credit cards

This b&b in sunny Carmel Valley has changed from a resort hotel to a country inn with conference center in recent years. Accommodations include garden/patio rooms, fireplace suites with wet bars and decks, and fireplace cottages with kitchens. All guest rooms are individually decorated in a blend of antiques, reproductions, and comfortable country pieces and have open-beamed ceilings and rustic-looking woods. Fresh coffee and tea, color cable TV, and flowers fresh from the garden are special touches for the guests' enjoyment. Guests may enjoy the pool, a hot spa, sauna, a new fitness center, and game area. The inn is just a short walk from village shops and restaurants. A complimentary breakfast is served in the conference-center dining room or in the room. Groups of up to thirty may be accommodated in the conference facilities.

Beach House

6360 Moonstone Beach Drive, Cambria, CA 93428
Phone: (805) 927-3136
Key: Home; 5 units; Moderate-Exp.; No smoking; No children under 12; Credit cards

This private, three-story, A-frame house is situated on picturesque Moonstone Beach. The five individually decorated guest rooms all boast private baths, antique oak furnishings, queen- or king-size beds, and breathtaking ocean views. Guests enjoy a sitting room on the ground floor as well as a second-floor common room that faces the ocean and has a large stone fireplace for chilly evenings. The buffet-style breakfast with fresh fruit and muffins is presented on the breakfast bar, and guests eat at the large dining-room table.

D'Urbano Bed & Breakfast

P.O. Box 1516, Cambria, CA 93428
Phone: (805) 927-8145
Key: Home; 2 units; Inexpensive; No smoking; No children; No credit cards

This two-story, Cape Cod–style home in a residential neighborhood overlooks the ocean and forest below. Tucked away in the pines, guests at the home b&b enjoy a peaceful patio as well as a living room with fireplace. The guest bedrooms are decorated comfortably and offer private baths. A full breakfast is included in the stay. This home b&b is just ten minutes from Hearst Castle.

The J. Patrick House, Cambria

The J. Patrick House

2990 Burton Drive, Cambria, CA 93428
Phone: (805) 927-3812
Key: Inn; 8 units; Moderate; No smoking; No children; Credit cards

This log home nestled in the pines is joined by an old-fashioned arbor and colorful garden to a private guest-room annex; together, they form this relaxing b&b retreat near the ocean. The log house contains an Early American pine- and oak-furnished living room with a cheery fireplace, where guests gather for wine and cheese each evening, as well as a sunny dining room, where the breakfast of freshly ground coffee, home-baked cinnamon rolls and muffins, and fresh fruit with condiments is served. The guest rooms are individually decorated and reflect the same comfortable, traditional motif. All accommodations have private baths and cozy fireplaces. Warm, personal service is the hallmark of this b&b.

Pickford House B&B

P.O. Box 1676, 2555 MacLeod Avenue, Cambria, CA 93428
Phone: (805) 927-8619
Key: Inn; 8 units; Moderate-Exp.; Limited smoking; Children OK; Credit cards

This contemporary structure with a turn-of-the-century flavor offers interesting antiques, a spacious 1860s pub area, and views of the Santa Lucia Mountains. The guest rooms, all with private baths featuring claw-foot tubs and pull-chain toilets, are named after silent-movie stars, with the decor to match. Some rooms offer fireplaces with antique mantles. The full breakfast is served downstairs in the parlor, as are afternoon wine or beer and hors d'oeuvres.

The Shaw House

2476 Main Street, Cambria, CA 93428
Phone: (805) 927-3222
Key: Inn; 6 units; Inexpensive-Mod.; Smoking OK; No children; No credit cards

An eighty-year-old coastal redwood tree fronts this picturesque Greek Revival home built in the 1870s. The inn is registered with the Historic House Association of America and is located across the street from a historic church and cemetery. A nature trail behind the inn leads to Santa Rosa Creek, yet the inn is also within walking distance of village shops and restaurants. The guest rooms at the inn are decorated to reflect a variety of themes, such as oriental, New England, and western. Rooms share three full baths, and all have in-room sherry and cable TV. A continental breakfast is served in the "Fireplace Room" each morning.

Darken Downs Equestre-Inn

Star Route Box 4562, San Miguel, CA 93451
Phone: (805) 467-3589
Key: Home; 2 units; Inexpensive; No smoking; No children; No credit cards

With or without horses, guests are welcome at this "equestrian" b&b nine miles north of Paso Robles in the small town of San Miguel. Two guest rooms are available in the recently built Spanish-style ranch house with Southwest accents. One accommodation is decorated in antiques and boasts a double sleigh bed; the other offers twin beds. The dining room of the house is the site of the morning continental fare; local wines and refreshments are offered in the afternoon. For those arriving "with horse," Darken Downs also offers horse boarding in its stucco box stalls or shaded paddocks and boasts a pasture and arena. Horses are boarded by the night or by the week at a reduced rate.

Almond View Inn, Paso Robles

Almond View Inn

912 Walnut Drive, Paso Robles, CA 93446
Phone: (805) 238-4220
Key: Inn; 3 units; Moderate; No smoking; No children under 16; Credit cards

This 1930s-built inn sits on a hilltop on spacious grounds surrounded by gracious oaks and overlooking blooming almond, cherry, pomegranate, apricot, and red-bud trees. The three-story classic, Mission Revival structure features balconies, wrought-iron railings, beamed ceilings, adobe-brick walls, and a red-clay tile roof. The inn's flower gardens host roses and a fountain; an acre below the inn is planned as a vineyard. The three guest rooms boast private baths, soft pastel colors, and either double, twin or queen-size beds. The full complimentary breakfast is served either in the dining room or in the breakfast nook; afternoon tea is offered under a spreading magnolia tree on the rose-garden patio. A sun deck and Jacuzzi are available to guests.

Roseleith Bed & Breakfast

1415 Vine Street, Paso Robles, CA 93446
Phone: (805) 238-5848
Key: Home; 3 units; Moderate-Exp.; No smoking; No children under 16; Credit cards

This 1892-built b&b is situated in a quaint Victorian residential area within easy walking distance of downtown boutiques, restaurants, and the graceful city park. The Stick-style Victorian house is surrounded by landscaped grounds that include a gazebo, fish pond, and carriage house with patio. The inn and guest rooms are furnished in eighteenth-century antiques with mahogany and cabbage rose chintz fabrics throughout. The individually decorated accommodations include two guest rooms that share a bath and one suite with private bath, sitting area, and king-size bed. Guests enjoy tea and scones or cake each afternoon in the front parlor; breakfast is served in the dining room. The generous morning meal includes a main course such as blintz soufflé or puffed apple pancake as well as freshly baked muffins, fruit, and juice.

Country House Inn

91 Main Street, Templeton, CA 93465
Phone: (805) 434-1598
Key: Inn; 6 units; Moderate; No smoking; Children on approval; Credit cards

This designated historic site is located on Main Street in the rustic town of Templeton, in the heart of the area's wine country. The 1886-built Victorian offers guest rooms with either king- or queen-size beds, private as well as shared baths, and antique furnishings. The main areas of the house feature two fireplaces for

199

relaxing or meeting with friends. A full breakfast is served in the formal dining room and boasts home-baked breads and fresh fruit. Guests at the inn may walk to the quaint shops of the western town and enjoy the inn's surrounding lawns and flower gardens.

Heritage Inn, San Luis Obispo

Heritage Inn

978 Olive Street, San Luis Obispo, CA 93401
Phone: (805) 544-7440
Key: Inn; 9 units; Moderate; No smoking; No children; Credit cards

Within walking distance to historic downtown yet yielding creek-side and mountain views, this turn-of-the-century inn offers an ideal central location. Furnished in warm antiques, cheerful wall coverings, and fresh flowers, each guest room hosts either a cozy window seat, fireplace, or walk-out terrace with views. Each room has its own vanity/sink area, and shared baths boast authentic claw-foot tubs, complete with bubblebath and pull-chain toilets. A large home-baked continental breakfast is served each morning in the fireside dining room, while wine and special hors d'oeuvres are offered each evening in the parlor.

The Guest House

120 Hart Lane, Arroyo Grande, CA 93420
Phone: (805) 481-9304
Key: Home; 3 units; Moderate; Limited smoking; No children; No credit cards

This house, constructed in the late 1850s by a northeastern sea family, is located in the quaint Old Town area. It is decorated with New England heirlooms, antiques, oriental rugs, and oil paintings. The three guest rooms share two baths and boast fresh garden bouquets. The comfortable living room with a grand piano is the site of afternoon tea or wine. A full New England–style breakfast is served in the parlor or on the garden terrace surrounded by an abundance of colorful blooms.

Rose Victorian Inn

789 Valley Road, Arroyo Grande, CA 93420
Phone: (805) 481-5566
Key: Inn/Cottages; 7 units; Expensive; No smoking; No children; Credit cards

This rose-colored, four-story inn complex built in 1885 consists of a main house and cottages that contain guest accommodations, as well as beautiful gardens with a rose arbor, gazebo, and koi ponds. The guest rooms, five in the house plus two cottages, offer king- or queen-size beds, nostalgic Victorian decor, and fresh roses from the garden. The inn's restaurant adjoins, serving gourmet dinners and Sunday brunches. A stay at the inn includes a full champagne breakfast served in the house's turn-of-the-century dining room and gourmet dinner at the restaurant. It has been rumored that the inn's special mascot is a "friendly" ghost from the past.

The Village Inn

407 El Camino Real, Arroyo Grande, CA 93420
Phone: (805) 489-5926
Key: Inn; 6 units; Moderate; No smoking; No children; Credit cards

The Village Inn, Arroyo Grande

The new and the old were combined to create this recently built Victorian b&b with a western influence. The inn, near U.S. 101, has an exterior with clapboard siding and bay windows designed to capture a rural "village" feel; the interior of the b&b blends warm colors with antique furnishings. The six guest rooms, all with private baths and queen-size beds, are located upstairs and are furnished individually in a variety of color schemes with such special touches as window seats, skylights, wall coverings and verandas. Soundproofing has been added. Guests may watch TV in the living room, and the dining room with its wood-plank floor and antique oak furniture is the site of a large farm-style breakfast each day. Late-afternoon refreshments also are offered at the inn.

Central Valley

California's Central Valley offers a wide spectrum of scenery from agricultural fields to snow-capped mountains, from deserts with creeks to nature's intriguing Devil's Post Piles, and from Death Valley to Mount Whitney. Visitors delight in ghost towns, ski resorts, and unlimited recreation. The Central Valley is so wide that you cannot see from one side to the other, and it boasts one of the richest agricultural areas in the world, an area growing everything from dry crops, such as cotton, to intensive crops, such as table grapes, wines, fruits, nuts, and vegetables. The southern portions of the valley are known for their oil production. The area is notable for its extreme weather variations, which range from hot temperatures in the summer months to tule fog conditions and colder weather in the wintertime. Bishop lies on the edge of the Sierra Nevada in the Owens Valley. The valley is flanked by the spectacular rise of these mountains and also boasts desertlike conditions. It is noted for its winter skiing and the Mammoth Mountain and June Lake recreational offerings. The Owens Valley is not noted, however, for its agricultural production due to the diversion of its water supply to Los Angeles.

The Matlick House

1313 Rowan Lane, Bishop, CA 93514
Phone: (619) 873-3133
Key: Inn; 5 units; Moderate; No smoking; No children under 15; No credit cards

This turn-of-the-century ranch house, originally owned by the apple orchard–ranching Matlick family, is nestled at the base of the valley between the Whites and the Sierra Nevada mountains. The two-story house with spacious first- and second-story porches is shaded by eighty-year-old elms and offers guests five suites, all with private baths, floral or country prints, handmade quilts, lace curtains, antiques, and ceiling fans. Several of the guest rooms boast views of the Sierras; "Mabel's Suite" enjoys a private exit to the second-story porch. Wine is served in the living room or on the screened veranda nightly, and a full country breakfast of freshly squeezed orange juice, biscuits, gravy, country fries, bacon, sausage, and eggs is served in the dining area. Picnic baskets and bicycles are provided for a nominal fee at this b&b surrounded by quiet and fresh mountain air.

Tatum's Bed & Breakfast

748 N. East Avenue, Reedley, CA 93654
Phone: (209) 638-4940
Key: Home; 1 unit; Inexpensive; No smoking; No children under 5; No credit cards

This brown-stucco home located in the "fruit basket of the world" is shaded by two giant sycamore trees. The house was built around 1916 and remodeled in 1952. The spacious yard of the b&b hosts ferns, fountains, and flower gardens; umbrella tables and lounge chairs are available to guests. The home offers just one accommodation to guests, the private "Golden Reflections Suite" with queen-size bed, color television, love seats, bath, kitchenette, air conditioning, and, of course, a bowl of fruit. Coffee, tea, or lemonade is available upon arrival, and the continental morning fare is served either in the suite or on the patio. Breakfast at this tranquil spot consists of juice, seasonal fruit, rolls, and beverages.

Valley View Citrus Ranch

14801 Avenue 428, Orosi, CA 93647
Phone: (209) 528-2275
Key: Home; 3 units; Inexpensive; Limited smoking; Children OK; No credit cards

Brilliant bougainvillea and citrus trees surround this hilltop, Spanish-style ranch house with dramatic views of the valley below. Guests may enjoy a full breakfast in the gazebo, play tennis on the clay court, hike, or relax on one of three patios. Afternoon refreshments include fresh fruit, fruit juice, or wine. Accommodations at the ranch b&b include a separate "Indian Room," with king-size bed and private bath, and rooms inside the house. All guest rooms boast air conditioning. The ranch b&b, south of Fresno, is just forty-five minutes from Sequoia National Park.

The Cort Cottage

P.O. Box 245, Three Rivers, CA 93271
Phone: (209) 561-4671
Key: Cottage; 1 unit; Moderate; Limited smoking; Children OK; No credit cards

Overlooking mountains, meadows of wildflowers, and fruit orchards is this b&b cottage nestled in a hillside near the main house. The contemporary wooden cottage, not far from the entrance to Sequoia National Park, was built in 1985 and offers a full kitchen and bath, a double bed, and comfortable sofa with double hide-a-bed. The b&b boasts a large, half-circle window in the living room and a unique, spacious deck constructed from the bottom of a wine barrel. Coffee and tea are stocked in the kitchen of the cottage, and the gracious innkeepers deliver the morning breakfast of juice, fruit, muffins or fruit bread, and cereal as well as fresh eggs for the guest to cook as desired. Wine and cheese may be shared each afternoon with the b&b's hosts.

Redwood Manor Bed & Breakfast

P.O. Box 582, 43811 So. Fork Drive, Three Rivers, CA 93271
Phone: (209) 561-4145/592-5656
Key: Home; 4 units; Moderate; Limited smoking; No children under 16; No credit cards

The South Fork River, with its wooden bridge and patches of wild berries, is just a short walk away from this retreat on two and one-half acres in the Sierra foothills. This spacious redwood contemporary home with spiral staircase, vaulted ceilings, and view windows was built by the innkeepers/owners and is filled with the family's travel momentos. Accommodations include both private and shared baths, cozy goose-down comforters, and designer-coordinated colors. The spacious "Redwood suite" boasts a high ceiling, king-size bed, sitting area, and private bath. The stay at Redwood Manor includes a full gourmet breakfast, with fresh fruits and homemade breads, as well as evening wine served in the common room or on the outside veranda.

Lemon Cove Bed & Breakfast Inn

33038 Sierra Highway, Lemon Cove, CA 93244
Phone: (209) 597-2555
Key: Inn; 5 units; Inexpensive-Mod.; No smoking; No children under 16; Credit cards

The scent of orange blossoms fill the air around this country b&b twenty-three miles from Sequoia National Park. The two-story, Colonial, stucco-and-wood house is surrounded by five acres of orange orchards, and, in season, guests may pick oranges for themselves. The five country-Victorian-decorated guest rooms share baths (except one) and boast cozy comforters, antiques, fresh flowers, and in-season fruit baskets. The "Chantilly Lace Room" offers a queen-size bed, whirlpool tub, private bath, balcony, and fireplace. Guests enjoy a spectacular mountain view from the veranda and a swimming pool. The full breakfast includes a "chef's specialty" such as cheesy scrambled eggs and large muffins, bacon, fruit salad, juice, and coffee and is served in the dining room or by the pool.

Larson's Bed 'n Breakfast

718 Philippine Street, Taft, CA 93268
Phone: (805) 765-2917
Key: Home; 2 units; Inexpensive; Limited smoking; No children; No credit cards

This custom-built, split-level home in the foothills has a sun deck with spectacular views and an olympic-size swimming pool. Guests also may enjoy a pool room with pool table and fireplace, a living room with fireplace, and a family room with TV and stereo. The guest rooms at this home b&b are furnished in Early American decor with four-posters, wall coverings, family portraits, shutters, rocking chairs, and ceiling fans. A continental breakfast featuring freshly baked breads and muffins is offered each morning, and wine and crackers are served in the evening. The innkeeper also runs a manicure-and-pedicure business from the premises and provides those services to guests for an additional fee.

SOUTHERN CALIFORNIA

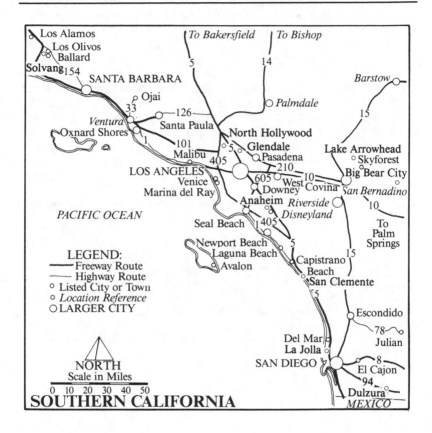

Los Alamos
Los Olivos
Ballard
Solvang 154
SANTA BARBARA

To Bakersfield   *To Bishop*

5   14

Ojai
33
Ventura
Oxnard Shores
126
Santa Paula
Palmdale
Barstow
15

North Hollywood
1   101
Malibu   405
Glendale
Pasadena
210
Lake Arrowhead
Skyforest
Big Bear City

LOS ANGELES
Venice
Marina del Ray
605   West
Downey   Covina
10
San Bernadino
10

PACIFIC OCEAN
Anaheim   *Riverside*
Disneyland
Seal Beach   405
To
Palm
Springs

Newport Beach   5
Laguna Beach
Avalon
Capistrano   15
Beach
San Clemente
5

LEGEND:
Freeway Route
Highway Route
○ Listed City or Town
○ *Location Reference*
○ LARGER CITY

Escondido
78
Julian

Del Mar
La Jolla
SAN DIEGO
8
El Cajon
94
Dulzura

NORTH
Scale in Miles
0 10 20 30 40 50

SOUTHERN CALIFORNIA

MEXICO

Known best as the home of Disneyland and the Hollywood stars, the "southland" also boasts spectacular swimming, surfing, and yachting from Santa Barbara to San Diego, mountain retreats, and desert playgrounds. Within this varietal expanse may be found serene country settings such as citrus-filled Ojai, the grapevineyard and horse-ranch areas of Los Olivos and Ballard, and the Danish community of Solvang. Artistic communities such as Laguna and Santa Barbara abound, as do several respected art museums including the Norton Simon and Getty museums. The urban areas offer lots of people and cars but theater, fine restaurants, shopping, and history as well. A trip through downtown Los Angeles and Olvera Street will give a glimpse of the area's rich past, as do the many historic communities with original missions and adobes, such as San Juan Capistrano and San Diego (with Zoo and Animal Park as well). Late-1880 California can be relived through the towns of Los Alamos and Julian. Recreation, history, beauty, and urban and rural settings all make up southern California, a bounty of travel choices.

Union Hotel

362 Bell Street, Los Alamos, CA 93440
Phone: (805) 344-2744
Key: Inn/Hotel; 14 units; Moderate; Smoking OK; No children; No credit cards

Agriculture and antique shops provide the setting for this restored 1880s hotel that boasts a busy family-style dinner trade downstairs. Guests get a tour of the area in a 1918 fifteen-passenger White touring car after breakfast and partake of wine and popcorn in the "saloon" each evening. A pool, Jacuzzi, and pool table are available. Rooms are open Friday, Saturday, and Sunday nights only.

The Ballard Inn

2436 Baseline, Ballard, CA 93463
Phone: (805) 688-7770
Key: Inn; 15 units; Expensive-Del.; Smoking OK; No children; Credit cards

This b&b inn, nestled in the historic town of Ballard within the lush Santa Ynez Valley, offers guests a blend of the old and new. The gabled inn, built in a nostalgic design with a multitude of fireplaces, offers four common rooms and fifteen guest rooms, each decorated in a theme consistent with the area's history yet containing the most modern conveniences. Three common rooms offer relaxation, wine, and a library, and the "William Ballard" dining room is the locale of breakfast. Guests also may dine in the room or on the veranda, and tea is served each day at 4:00 P.M. Each of the guest rooms at the inn features a private bath and individual touches that include balconies, American antiques, quilts, antique-doll collections, Chumash Indian designs, and unique circular windows; several rooms have stone fireplaces.

Larry & Linda's Bed & Breakfast

1841 Cottonwood Street, Ballard, CA 93463
Phone: (805) 688-2400
Key: Home; 1 unit; Moderate; Smoking OK; Children OK; No credit cards

This home in the quaint historic town of Ballard is situated on one-half acre of beautifully landscaped grounds. Just three miles from Solvang, the innkeepers reflect the Danish influence with a full breakfast of Danish pastries or *aebelskivers*, Danish sausage, fruit, eggs, and coffee. The guest room boasts a queen-size bed and double bed and has a private bath. Afternoon refreshments are served; families are welcome.

Cottonwood Meadow

2601 Baseline Avenue, Solvang, CA 93463
Phone: (805) 688-2602
Key: Home; 3 units; Moderate; No smoking; No children under 10; No credit cards

This ranch-style b&b is situated on five country acres in the Danish community of Solvang and boasts horses, sheep, chickens, and more than 300 assorted trees. The spacious, two-story cedar house offers three bedrooms for guests: a large room upstairs, with private bath and entrance, television, queen-size bed, and twin bed, and two rooms downstairs. The breakfast of Danish pastries, blueberry muffins, two types of fresh fruit, and juice is served in the formal dining room or on the outside deck. Guests enjoy the sunken conversation pit in the living room decorated with antiques and Navajo rugs.

El Ranchito

1451 Alamo Pintado Road, Solvang, CA 93463
Phone: (805) 688-9517/688-9360
Key: Cottages; 2 units; Expensive; No smoking; No children; No credit cards

A few miles out of Solvang is this ranch b&b surrounded by oaks, vineyards, olive trees, and bursts of iris, lavender, and roses. The two Mediterranean-style cottages for guests are furnished in antiques and country pieces and offer desks, sofas, overstuffed chairs, fresh flowers, and chilled wine. The "Villa Amore" cottage also has a woodstove and all the makings for a cozy fire. Orange juice and a thermos of coffee are delivered to the cottage around 7:00 A.M., and breakfast, served inside the cottage or on the cottage patio, is offered whenever the guest desires. The full fare consists of Danish pastries, sausage, homemade muffins, fresh eggs, and fruit. This tranquil spot not only has its own year-round stream but also fourteen resident "celebrity" llamas and three alpacas. A two-night minimum stay is required.

Petersen Village Inn

1576 Mission Drive, Solvang, CA 93463
Phone: (805) 688-3121/(800) 321-8985
Key: Inn/Hotel; 40 units; Moderate-Exp.; Limited smoking; No children under 5; Credit cards

This Danish-style hotel is a part of a "village" in the heart of Solvang that has been gradually completed over the last few years, the b&b hotel being the most recent addition. The b&b rooms are

Petersen Village Inn, Solvang

scattered throughout the "village" on the second floor of many of the dozen village buildings and offer views of the quaint Danish streets, shops, and courtyard. Each of the hotel minisuites is decorated individually, and many have wallpapers, authentic canopy beds, sitting areas with couches, down pillows, balconies, and fresh flowers. A complimentary breakfast of hard rolls, pastry, coffee, and juice is served in the Petersen Square courtyard bakery each morning. This family-owned hotel offers a European touch and personal services as well as larger hotel amenities such as dining and conference facilities.

The Trout Farm

2844 Covered Wagon Road, Solvang, CA 93463
Phone: (805) 688-9517/688-9360
Key: Home; 2 units; Expensive; No smoking; No children; No credit cards

Just two miles from the Danish town of Solvang is this former fishery b&b. The farm now consists of a quarter-acre main pond, with docks for fishing and sunbathing, as well as giant eucalyptus and elms and flowing lawns with croquet. The ninety-year-old main house in red and white boasts large porches for relaxing as well as an 1895-furnished living room and dining room. The two individually furnished guest suites offer their own fireplaces, baths, and private entrances. The very personal service at this home b&b includes a full breakfast featuring such main entrees as oven pancakes with syrups or vegetable quiche. All-the-time refreshments at the inn include iced tea, hot chocolate, and special homemade cookies.

n Inn

vina Street, Santa Barbara, CA 93101
Jne: (805) 965-6532
Key: Inn/Hotel; 44 units; Moderate-Exp.; Smoking OK; Children OK; Credit cards

Conveniently located downtown, this four-building hotel consists of both the old and new. A majority of guest-room offerings are "minisuites" complemented by such amenities as kitchens, patios, and gardens. A full English country breakfast is served, and an afternoon wine tasting is featured. Corporate rates and long-term accommodations are available.

The Bath Street Inn

1720 Bath Street, Santa Barbara, CA 93101
Phone: (805) 682-9680
Key: Inn; 7 units; Moderate-Exp; Smoking OK; No children; Credit cards

This restored, 1885 Queen Anne–Victorian inn, situated in a tree-lined residential area downtown, provides guests with a unique common-lounge area on the gabled third floor. Sunny-patio breakfast dining is enjoyed in the rear gardens. The inn offers complimentary bicycles and afternoon refreshments of wine, lemonade, cheese, and crackers. Guest rooms with mountain views at the inn feature private baths, polished hardwood floors, traditional wallpapers, antiques, and fresh flowers. A library and TV room have been added for guests' enjoyment, as has a summerhouse for outdoor socializing.

Bayberry Inn

111 West Valerio Street, Santa Barbara, CA 93101
Phone: (805) 682-3199
Key: Inn; 8 units; Moderate-Exp.; No smoking; No children under 13; Credit cards

212

Built as a French ambassador's residence in 1886, the inn has a distinctive shingled exterior with blue-and-white trim and shutters. The inn features glorious flower arrangements, five cozy fireplaces (four within guest rooms), a sun deck, and interesting antiques from around the world. Guest rooms feature imported canopy beds and have sitting areas and romantic turn-of-the-century decor; one guest room even offers a Jacuzzi. Wine and hors d'oeuvres are served in the evening, and a full gourmet breakfast is graciously served on fine china and silver.

Blue Quail Inn and Cottages

1908 Bath Street, Santa Barbara, CA 93101
Phone: (805) 687-2300
Key: Inn/Cottages; 8 units; Moderate; Limited smoking; No children under 13; Credit cards

Antiques and a country motif decorate the individual rooms and suites of this redwood-frame inn and its four cottages. The cottages feature their own living room, kitchen, and bath, and all suites have their own parlor. Bicycles and picnic lunches are available with prior notice. In addition to the complimentary breakfast of freshly baked popovers and muffins, guests enjoy cold lemonade or spiced apple cider in the evening.

Brinkerhoff Inn

523 Brinkerhoff Avenue, Santa Barbara, CA 93101
Phone: (805) 963-7844/(800) 237-8262 (CA)
Key: Inn/Cottage; 6 units; Moderate-Exp.; No smoking; No children under 13; Credit cards

Nestled in a nostalgic block packed with antique stores, boutiques, art galleries, Victorian homes, and flower gardens is this new inn with the Victorian landmark avenue's namesake, Brinkerhoff. The 1887 house boasts elegant window dressings that hint of the innkeeper's other business, old-fashioned costume making. The totally renovated inn boasts antique furnishings, coordinated fabrics, and wall coverings as well as plumed hats and

213

Brinkerhoff Inn, Santa Barbara

fancy window decorations throughout. The guest accommodations are uniquely appointed and feature the airy, treetop "Swan's Nest," mountain views from "Amelia's Room," and a separate two-room cottage. The stay at this downtown b&b includes breakfast under the shady avocado tree, afternoon tea with tasty desserts, a trolley ride, and a memento photo of the guest in historical costume.

The Cheshire Cat

36 West Valerio Street, Santa Barbara, CA 93101
Phone: (805) 569-1610
Key: Inn; 11 units; Expensive-Del.; No smoking; No children; No credit cards

Two vintage homes have been lovingly restored to create a "fairy-tale" b&b with delicate Laura Ashley wall coverings and fabrics, high ceilings, bay windows, and lots of private nooks. The inn offers eleven guest rooms, all with private baths, English antiques, and king- or queen-size brass beds, and some rooms feature a fireplace, patio, or spa. Flowers, chocolates, and liqueurs are placed in each room. Names of the guest rooms are taken from *Alice in Wonderland*, and especially notable is Alice's own suite. The breakfast buffet is served at the large oak dining table, and local wines are offered each evening. A relaxing courtyard patio is nestled between the two homes of the inn, and a spa is built into the private gazebo. Bicycles are available for touring.

The Cottage

840 Mission Canyon Road, Santa Barbara, CA 93105
Phone: (805) 682-4461/682-4997
Key: Home/Cottage; 2 units; Inexpensive-Mod.; No smoking; Children on approval; No credit cards

This home with a rear, paneled cottage is located amid ancient oak trees and is within walking distance of the mission. The tastefully decorated cottage unit provides a double bed with single rollaway available, a living room with TV, and a shower/bath. A small refrigerator is stocked with milk, orange juice, coffee, tea, fresh fruit, and baked goods for a self-catered breakfast. The suite inside the home contains two bedrooms, sitting room, private bath, and private entrance. Guests enjoy the same self-catered breakfast in the suite. Only last-minute reservations accepted are those for a single night.

The Glenborough Inn, Santa Barbara

The Glenborough Inn

1327 Bath Street, Santa Barbara, CA 93101
Phone: (805) 966-0589
Key: Inn/Cottage; 9 units; Moderate-Del.; Limited smoking; No children under 13; Credit cards

This 1906 craftsman house and the 1880s summer cottage kitty-corner across the street provide the nine guest accommodations at the inn. The main house offers a cozy parlor with wood-burning stove, comfortable antiques, oak floors with oriental rugs, and games and reading material. Four upstairs rooms share a bath and feature nostalgic, turn-of-the-century, decor; the main house now offers a private garden suite with fireplace, sitting room, private entrance and deck, and patio with fountain. The cottage offers two spacious suites with canopies, fireplaces, and private baths as well as two guest rooms with private baths and pretty antiques. Guests are treated to a full gourmet breakfast prepared from scratch and served in the room or the gardens. A fully enclosed outdoor hot tub may be enjoyed in total privacy, and wine and hors d'oeuvres are offered either by fireside or in the gardens each evening. Bicycles are available.

The Inn at 222

222 W. Valerio, Santa Barbara, CA 93101
Phone: (805) 687-7216
Key: Inn; 6 units; Moderate-Del.; Limited smoking; No children; Credit cards

This turn-of-the-century inn, luxuriously restored to its late-1800s elegance, is nestled a few blocks from town on a large, deep lot with trees and flowering gardens. Calling itself the "Bed & Breakfast Conference Center of Santa Barbara," this b&b is able to host up to thirty-six people in its well-appointed common area containing antiques, a fireplace, and clips for charts; hosts will provide services for meetings if prearranged. Guests may choose from six unique guest rooms that offer polished hardwood floors or deep carpet, rich woodwork, wall coverings, fresh flowers and fruit, and private bathrooms. The "French Consul's Room" features a spa for two under a skylight, a stained-glass window, and a mountain-view balcony. The morning meal is served in the dining room or on the large, covered redwood deck outside; breakfast trays are available. Breakfast includes homemade granola, fresh juice, fruits, and homemade breads and jam. Guests may borrow the inn's bicycles for a fifteen-minute ride to the beach.

Long's Sea View Lodge

317 Piedmont Road, Santa Barbara, CA 93105
Phone: (805) 687-2947
Key: Home; 1 unit; Moderate; No smoking; No children under 10;
No credit cards

This home b&b, located near Santa Barbara attractions, offers a rural atmosphere within the city. A full breakfast is served on a forty-five-foot-long patio that affords views of the ocean, the Channel Islands, and the family orchard. The large, airy guest room has an antique brass double bed, antique furnishings, and a private bath and entrance; a third person may be accommodated in the adjoining den. Wine is served on arrival, and guests may enjoy the patio, gardens, and spa.

The Old Yacht Club Inn

431 Corona Del Mar, Santa Barbara, CA 93103
Phone: (805) 962-1277/962-3989
Key: Inn; 9 units; Moderate-Exp.; Limited smoking; No children under 14; Credit cards

Just one-half block from the beach is Santa Barbara's first b&b, composed now of two old residences that sit side by side. The original b&b structure was the city's yacht club in the 1920s, and the 1925-built home next door became an inn expansion in 1983. Together the comfortably decorated homes in antiques and colorful fabrics offer nine guest rooms filled with antiques, homey touches, decanters of sherry, and oriental rugs; four have sitting areas, private baths, and private entries. Guests may sip sherry by the parlor fire or on the porch, and the inn is well known for its gourmet breakfasts featuring omelettes, quiches, frittatas, or French toast. Candlelight dinners may be arranged at the inn, and guests are able to use the inn's bicycles, beach towels, and beach chairs.

The Olive House

1604 Olive Street, Santa Barbara, 93101
Phone: (805) 962-4902
Key: Inn; 6 units; Moderate; No smoking; No children; Credit cards

This 1904 California Craftsman home offers six guest rooms with private baths. The sunny accommodations boast French doors, ocean views, and decks for sunning as well as down comforters, antique furnishings, and fresh flowers. Guests may gather in the spacious, paneled living room with its fireplace or on the large sun deck with views of the mountains and ocean for evening wine and hors d'oeuvres. A full country breakfast is served in the dining room. The inn's convenient location is just minutes from shops and a five-minute drive to the beach.

Ocean View Guest House

P.O. Box 20065, Santa Barbara, CA 93102
Phone: (805) 966-6659
Key: Home; 1-2 units; Inexpensive; No smoking; Children OK; No credit cards

This private home, located in a quiet suburban neighborhood, is within walking distance of the ocean. The guest room with antiques adjoins a private bath and paneled den with television. Guests may breakfast on the backyard patio with ocean views. A continental fare plus eggs and cheese or quiche is served on china. Well equipped for children, the fenced yard is grassy and sports a playhouse complete with toys. A two-night-minimum stay is required.

The Parsonage

1600 Olive Street, Santa Barbara, CA 93101
Phone: (805) 962-9336
Key: Inn; 6 units; Moderate-Exp.; Smoking OK; No children under 13; Credit cards

This Queen Anne–Victorian house was built as a parsonage for the Trinity Episcopal Church in 1892. Located in the upper east residential area, it is near downtown attractions. A private solarium in the master suite offers views of the city and Channel Islands. Oriental rugs, antiques, and bird's-eye-redwood woodwork enhance the former rectory interiors. The special "Honeymoon Suite" boasts a bedroom, solarium, and private bath along with a king-size canopy bed, stained-glass windows, and outstanding views.

Red Rose Inn, Santa Barbara

Red Rose Inn

1416 Castillo, Santa Barbara, CA 93101
Phone: (805) 966-1470
Key: Inn; 6 units; Moderate-Exp.; No smoking; No children under 14; Credit cards

This elegantly restored 1800s inn boasts high arches, stained-glass windows, bay windows, and old-fashioned gardens with more than sixty rose bushes. The interior of the b&b offers turn-of-the-century wallpapers, prints, and furnishings, and guests may relax in the parlor, on the sun porch, or in the dining room with its romantic fireplace. Guest rooms offer both private and shared baths, antiques, oriental rugs, roses from the garden, and some bay windows and mountain views. The continental breakfast featuring homemade breads and muffins may be enjoyed by the fire-place, in the room, or on the sun porch; wine is served in the evening. Special touches at the inn include sherry and coffee or tea always available on the sideboard, terry robes in all the rooms and baths, and picnic lunches provided on request.

Simpson House Inn

121 E. Arrellaga, Santa Barbara, CA 93101
Phone: (805) 963-7067
Key: Inn; 6 units; Moderate-Exp.; No smoking; No children under 12; Credit cards

This 1874-built b&b, honored with a "Structure of Merit" award, is nestled on a secluded acre of grounds with tall hedges, English gardens, curving paths, lawns, and mature shade trees and is within walking distance of town. The restored inn, appointed throughout with tasteful antiques, includes a spacious sitting room with library and fireplace and an adjoining formal dining room. French doors lead to a garden veranda with white wicker seating. The six guest rooms, several named for the original Simpson family owners, offer special features such as English laces, oriental rugs, antiques, and queen- or king-size beds; all but one unit boasts a private bath. The "Robert and Julia Simpson Room" features a private sitting area and French doors that open onto a spacious garden deck, and the "Parlor Room" boasts a bay window, fireplace, and small library. The morning meal is served on the veranda, the brick patio, or private decks or in the dining room and consists of freshly squeezed orange juice, teas and coffee, fresh fruit, and a variety of breads, muffins, and cereals. The inn offers evening wine and hors d'oeuvres as well as afternoon tea on request.

The Tiffany Inn

1323 De la Vina Street, Santa Barbara, CA 93101
Phone: (805) 963-2283
Key: Inn; 5 units; Moderate-Exp.; No smoking; No children under 13; Credit cards

This 1898 Victorian home has been completely restored with its diamond-paned windows, wood staircase, and authentic bath intact. Guests enjoy an old-fashioned garden with wicker furniture and a lattice-covered porch as well as evening wine and cheese before a parlor fire. Guest rooms with turn-of-the-century furnishings, queen-size beds, and several fireplaces offer both shared and private baths. A breakfast of fresh fruit, juice, croissants, pastries, and coffee or tea is served each morning in the dining room or on the old-fashioned porch.

Upham Hotel

1404 De la Vina Street, Santa Barbara, CA 93101
Phone: (805) 962-0058
Key: Inn/Hotel/Cottages; 38 units; Moderate; Smoking OK; Children OK; Credit cards

Claiming to be the "oldest hotel in continual use in southern California," the Upham consists of an 1871-vintage structure with both turn-of-the-century and 1920s additions. Reminiscent of its early origins, a third-floor widow's walk has a spyglass once used to spot boats arriving with hotel patrons. Guests enjoy a game of lawn croquet and verandas that open onto the gardens. Guest rooms are all in Victorian decor; some feature private yards, porches, or fireplaces. The master suite boasts a large indoor Jacuzzi. Croissants, juice, fruit, and toast, as well as muffins on the weekend, are served on the porch and in the comfortable lobby each morning; complimentary wine is offered at the lobby wine bar from 3:00 in the afternoon until closing each day.

Villa Rosa

15 Chapala Street, Santa Barbara, CA 93101
Phone: (805) 966-0851
Key: Inn/Hotel; 18 units; Moderate-Del.; Smoking OK; No children under 14; Credit cards

Claiming "eighteen rooms just eighty-four steps from the beach," this hotel-type b&b is a contemporary rendition with rough-hewn beams, plantation shutters, and louvered doors. A lounge adjoins the pool and spa in the garden courtyard. Included is a continental breakfast and wine and cheese. Light and airy guest rooms and suites, all with private baths, boast pastel color schemes and a combination of contemporary and Spanish Colonial furnishings.

Bushman Bed & Breakfast

1220 No. Montgomery Street, Ojai, CA 93023
Phone: (805) 646-4295
Key: Home; 3 units; Inexpensive; No smoking; Children OK; No credit cards

This 2,900-square-foot Spanish-style home is located on the edge of town among the oaks of the foothills with the mountains as a picturesque backdrop. The guest rooms share one and one-half baths and feature English wallpapers, a pineapple four-poster, and a patchwork quilt. The living room offers fine books and a fireplace. A side patio with a fountain is a restful choice for the morning breakfast, which includes apple-raisin bran muffins and sliced oranges or fresh orange juice from the family orchard.

Casa de La Luna Bed & Breakfast

710 La Luna Avenue, Ojai, CA 93023
Phone: (805) 646-4528
Key: Home; 4 units; Moderate-Exp.; No smoking; No children under 10; No credit cards

This elegant, 5,000-square-foot, Spanish-style hacienda offers four private guest accommodations surrounded by seven acres of oaks and the locally well-known "Gardens of Perpetual Spring." Guests are invited to tour the entire tranquil estate, in which they may pick fresh fruit year-round and view both the exotic plant nursery with its more than 1,000 plants and gardens with meandering pathways through colorful blooms. The overnight accommodations include "The Estate Suite" with fireplace, king-size bed and private bath. Guests "choose" their own full gourmet breakfast from a generous check list; the morning fare is served either in the large, formal dining room or in the cozy kitchen. Guests are encouraged to enjoy the living room of the house with its wooden carved mantel and fireplace and etched-glass windows, the extensive library with antique desk, and a relaxing atrium. The "Gallery of Fine Arts" just across from the hacienda displays original art by the owners/innkeepers.

Ojai Bed & Breakfast

921 Patricia Court, Ojai, CA 93023
Phone: (805) 646-8337
Key: Home; 2 units; Moderate; No smoking; No children under 13; No credit cards

This private residence, located in the quiet and beautiful town of Ojai, offers mountain-view rooms decorated in Early American, an impressive rose garden, and homemade muffins and organic jams made from produce grown in the garden. The full breakfast also includes eggs, cereal, or French toast.

Glen Tavern Inn

134 N. Mill Street, Santa Paula, CA 93060
Phone: (805) 525-6658
Key: Inn/Hotel; 41 units; Inexpensive-Exp.; Smoking OK; Children OK; Credit cards

Built in 1911 as a hotel convenient to the now historic "Depot," this three-story English Tudor inn features peaked gables, rich woodwork, and a 1900s European decor in forest greens and beiges. The recently restored hotel has served as a backdrop for several motion pictures and television shows. The forty-one guest rooms, all with private baths, are individually furnished and decorated with wall coverings, brass overhead fans, and antique beds. Some accommodations feature Jacuzzis. A full breakfast of omelettes (a different one each day), fresh fruit, juice, and coffee is included in the stay. A fine restaurant is also on the premises.

The Lemon Tree Inn, Santa Paula

The Lemon Tree Inn

299 West Santa Paula Street, Santa Paula, CA 93060
Phone: (805) 525-7747
Key: Inn; 4 units; Moderate; No smoking; No children; Credit cards

This turn-of-the-century California farmhouse is situated on a peaceful acre of land filled with fruit trees and avocados and featuring a brick-and-lattice patio. The spacious guest rooms, with shared and private baths, are furnished in an assortment of antiques, wicker, brass, and 1920s decor as well as patchworks, calicos, and delicate pastels. The breakfast features juice, seasonal fruit, homemade breads, and jams (from the garden); it is served on the patio or in the dining room. Wine and hors d'oeuvres are served in the living room each evening, and picnic lunches are available with prior notice. Guests often depart with a bag of avocados from the orchards.

Bella Maggiore Inn

67 S. California Street, Ventura, CA 93001
Phone: (805) 652-0277/(800) 241-3848/(800) 523-8479 (CA)
Key: Inn; 17 units; Moderate-Del.; Smoking OK; No children;
Credit cards

As a part of the Ventura Historic Walking Tour, this b&b stands out with its classical Italian facade of stone and umbrella awnings. The downstairs area of the inn, its lobby, features antiques, a baby grand piano, and fresh flowers from the garden. Guests may enjoy the full breakfast here as well as afternoon refreshments and appetizers. The picturesque patio courtyard with Roman fountain is surrounded by flowers and greenery and is a breakfast locale as well. The guest rooms at the inn feature private baths, ceiling fans, shutters, fresh flowers, candy, Italian Capuan beds, and a variety of color schemes. Some of the guest rooms open onto the patio or sun deck at this European-style inn just blocks from the beach.

La Mer

411 Poli Street, Ventura, CA 93001
Phone: (805) 643-3600
Key: Inn; 5 units; Moderate-Exp.; No smoking; No children under 14; Credit cards

This 1890-built, Cape Cod–style b&b is nestled on a hillside a few blocks from town and grants inspiring views of the ocean. The distinctive guest rooms, all with private baths, are each a European adventure with such offerings as the "Madame Pompadour" room with bay window, balcony, and woodstove; the Austrian "Wienderwald" with sunken tub; and the Flemish "Peter Paul Reubens" with an ocean-view veranda. The guest rooms feature antiques, cozy European comforters, and complimentary wine; all but one room has a private entrance. A breakfast buffet featuring apple strudel or homemade cake is served in the Bavar-

La Mer, Ventura

ian-style dining room from 8:00 to 9:30 each morning; the inn also serves wine, champagne, sparkling apple cider, or Austrian beer. Guests at this old-world b&b have use of a turn-of-the-century lounge.

Casa Larronde

P.O. Box 86, 22000 Pacific Coast Highway, Malibu, CA 90265
Phone: (213) 456-9333
Key: Home; 1 unit; Moderate; Smoking OK; Children OK; No credit cards

A private beach and movie-star neighbors are attractive and unique ingredients of this home b&b in famous Malibu. The spacious, two-story home offers a living room with ocean-view windows and a guest suite with fireplace, minikitchen, TV, sitting area, beamed ceilings, ash paneling, and floor-to-ceiling ocean-view windows. The guest suite also boasts a forty-foot private deck with views of the bay and pier. The breakfast may be enjoyed on the deck, and complimentary champagne and hors d'oeuvres are offered in the evening. The b&b is closed during the summer and when the hosts are traveling.

The Venice Beach House

No. 15, Thirtieth Avenue, Venice, CA 90291
Phone: (213) 823-1966

Key: Inn; 9 units; Inexpensive-Del.; No smoking; No children; Credit cards

The 1911 historic-landmark building offers guest rooms and suites, some with balconies, fireplaces, sitting rooms, whirlpool tubs, or side-by-side claw-foot tubs. All of the charming guest accommodations feature antiques, and many have canopies and antique quilts. The generous continental breakfast is served in bed, in the parlor, or on the veranda with ocean views. In the evening, guests share refreshments in front of a cozy fire or on the veranda watching the summer sun set. Picnic baskets are available for exploring or beach going at this inn next to the beach.

Eastlake Inn, Los Angeles

Eastlake Inn

1442 Kellam Avenue, Los Angeles, CA 90026
Phone: (213) 250-1620
Key: Inn; 5 units; Inexpensive-Exp.; No smoking; No children under 12; Credit cards

This authentically restored 1887 inn on a downtown hilltop began as a grand duplex for two wealthy widows. The Eastlake-style b&b is in the middle of the city's first historic-preservation area and is surrounded by other fine Victorian restoration examples. The interiors are furnished in museum-quality antiques and feature red pine floors and stained glass. The guest rooms share baths with luxurious claw-foot tubs and chenille robes and are decorated in interesting antiques, canopies, wicker, and beveled glass; a three-room honeymoon suite with private bath has recently been added. The generous breakfast is served on fine china in the dining room or guest room or even in bed. Champagne and wine are offered on arrival, and hors d'oeuvres are served each evening. Special weekend packages at the inn include limousine tours for chocolate lovers, hot-air balloons, and mysteries—to name just a few!

Salisbury House

2273 W. 20th Street, Los Angeles, CA 90018
Phone: (213) 737-7817
Key: Inn; 5 units; Moderate; Limited smoking; No children under 11; Credit cards

Just minutes from downtown Los Angeles is this 1909 California Craftsman home-turned-inn that features original stained and leaded glass, wood-beamed ceilings, wood paneling, and antique-filled rooms. The inn, in a quiet residential area, offers five individual guest rooms with turn-of-the-century wall coverings, bay windows, Victorian furniture, and eyelet and lace as well as private and shared baths. The third floor "Attic Suite" comprises 600-square-feet of area with a sitting room, claw-foot tub, pine floors, and gabled ceilings. A full breakfast with such delicacies as raspberry tea, almond coffee, quiche or apple puffed pancakes, and fresh fruit cobblers is served in the formal, wood-paneled dining room in buffet fashion. A wine rack is stocked with complimentary port, sherry, and burgundy.

Terrace Manor

1353 Alvarado Terrace, Los Angeles, CA 90006
Phone: (213) 381-1478
Key: Inn; 5 units; Moderate; No smoking; No children under 13; Credit cards

This 1902-built National Historic Landmark home in downtown Los Angeles contains its original stained- and leaded-glass windows, polished hardwood floors, and rich paneled walls. The Tudor-Craftsman home, formerly owned by soap-opera stars and writers and featured in TV movies and commercials, is filled with antiques and period furniture and has a hunter green, rose, and burgundy color scheme. The five guest rooms have private baths, some rare antiques, authentic wallcoverings, and some brass and iron beds. The stay here includes a full breakfast with such delicacies as eggs Florentine and tarts and is served in the dining room or in the garden. In the late afternoon guests gather in the parlor or library for wine and hors d'oeuvres. As a special treat, innkeepers are happy to make reservations for guests at the Magic Castle, a magicians' club that you cannot enter unless a member-magician invites you.

Belair

941 N. Frederic, Burbank, CA 91505
Phone: (818) 848-9227
Key: Home; 4 units; Inexpensive; Smoking OK; No children under 12; No credit cards

"Beautiful downtown Burbank" is the location of this home b&b in a quiet residential area just two miles from the Universal and NBC studios. The reasonable home b&b offers both private- and shared-bath accommodations for up to ten adults. Belair also offers a studio apartment and a guest house with kitchens and private baths. Guests may enjoy either a continental or full breakfast.

Shroff B&B Home

1114 Park Avenue, Glendale, CA 91205
Phone: (818) 507-0774
Key: Home; 1 unit; Inexpensive; Limited smoking; Children OK; No credit cards

This Spanish-style house on a residential street offers a pleasant rear garden with patio, gazebo, and small fruit orchard. The one guest accommodation is decorated in 1930s walnut furniture and shares a bath. A bar refrigerator is for guests' use, and a TV is available in the living room. A continental breakfast is served in the dining room between 7:00 A.M. and 9:00 A.M. and includes fresh goodies from the orchard. An evening snack is sometimes offered. Business travelers are encouraged at this budget-priced b&b; no personal checks are accepted.

La Maida House

11159 La Maida Street, North Hollywood, CA 91601
Phone: (818) 769-3857
Key: Inn; 10 units; Moderate-Del.; No smoking; No children; No credit cards

This 7,000-square-foot, 1920s villa in a quiet residential neighborhood is surrounded by flower gardens and fountains; guests also enjoy its gazebo, grape-arbored patios, swan pond with a pair of black swans, a reflecting pool, and water gardens. The interiors of the old-world mansion are filled with antiques, oriental rugs, stained glass, and rich mahogany. The ten guest rooms and suites at the inn feature private baths, some with claw-foot tubs or Jacuzzis; canopies; private patios or gardens; and rich antiques or wicker furniture. New additions to the rooms include private-line telephones and refrigerators. Early morning coffee or tea and the newspaper are delivered to the room, and the continental breakfast is served between 8:00 A.M. and 9:00 A.M. Evening apértifs are offered, and guests also may arrange for picnic baskets, pretheater supper, or a four-course dinner—all prepared by the inn's award-winning, gourmet chef. The inn has a new gift shop.

Donnymac Irish Inn

119 No. Meridith, Pasadena, CA 91106
Phone: (818) 440-0066
Key: Inn; 5 units; Moderate; No smoking; No children under 11; No credit cards

Donnymac Irish Inn, Pasadena

This two-story, turn-of-the-century inn carries its Irish theme throughout with its "Shamrock Corner" gift shop, "Blarney Place" lounge, and a waterfall area called the "Shannon Retreat." Guest rooms boast fresh flowers, fruit, and a "wee bit o' nod" decanter. The breakfast fare is served in the room, in the dining room, or on the mountain-view "Garden Balcony." Special offerings at the inn include a gazebo-housed spa, picnic baskets, and pickup service for air, train, and bus travelers. A complimentary bottle of champagne is offered for birthdays, anniversaries, and honeymoons.

Anaheim Country Inn

856 S. Walnut, Anaheim, CA 92802
Phone: (714) 778-0150
Key: Inn; 8 units; Moderate; No smoking; No children under 13; Credit cards

This Princess Anne–style house with sweeping front porch and grounds filled with avocado trees and roses was originally built in 1910. Guests may relax in the quiet of this residential neighborhood—just minutes from Disneyland—on one of three porches; in the large Victorian parlor with beveled-glass windows, an 1890 pump organ, Victrola, and cozy fireplace; or in the quiet upstairs reading room. The nine guest rooms and their private and shared baths, located both upstairs and down, are decorated individually with iron, wicker, or poster beds and early 1900s furnishings. The "Garden Room" has an outside entrance to the garden with spa. The sunny dining room is the locale of the generous full breakfast; late-afternoon snacks are offered on the parlor/library table.

The Seal Beach Inn and Gardens

212 5th Street, Seal Beach, CA 90740
Phone: (213) 493-2416
Key: Inn/Hotel; 23 units; Moderate-Del.; No smoking; Children on approval; Credit cards

This romantic, classic country inn with lush, colorful gardens sits in the charming village of Seal Beach. In a quiet residential neighborhood one block from the beach, the old-world b&b with blue canopies, window boxes, shutters, and brick courtyard offers twenty-three guest rooms, no two alike. Most of the guest rooms have kitchens and sitting areas, and all have private baths, antiques, TV, and telephones. Guest enjoy a library with tiled fireplace, brass chandeliers, an ornate antique tin ceiling, lace curtains, and vintage furnishings. The generous morning fare is served in the tearoom, by the poolside, or in the gardens that are dotted with interesting art and remain abloom year-round. Special packages are available.

Doryman's Inn

2102 W. Ocean Front, Newport Beach, CA 92663
Phone: (714) 675-7300
Key: Inn/Hotel; 10 units; Deluxe; Smoking OK; No children; Credit cards

This 1892-vintage hotel located on the ocean has been totally renovated and decorated in carefully selected antique furnishings and wall coverings. Each individually decorated guest room boasts a fireplace and marble sunken bath. A decanter of sherry awaits guests in the room, and the continental breakfast is served in the parlor each morning. The inn restaurant furnishes dinner in the room or parlor upon request.

The Little Inn on the Bay, Newport Beach

The Little Inn on the Bay

617 Lido Park Drive, Newport Beach, CA 92663
Phone: (714) 673-8800
Key: Inn/Hotel; 30 units; Expensive-Del.; Smoking OK; Children OK; Credit cards

This hotel b&b with marina has just been renovated to a village-style hostelry a short stroll from the quaint shops of the Cannery and Lido Village. Pretty beaches are just a few blocks away. Each of the thirty guest rooms offers a view of the water and has soundproofing, air conditioning, and individual decor that reflects an 1800s New England feel in antique reproductions. Several rooms have wet bars, refrigerators, and microwave ovens, and all accommodations have private baths. A complimentary continental breakfast may be enjoyed in the room or on the scenic dock-side patio with views of the boats and ducks. Daily complimentary services at the inn include a boat cruise of the bay from the inn's own dock, wine and hors d'oeuvres in the afternoon, a pedicab tour of Cannery Village and an after-dinner snack. Guests also enjoy bicycles, board games, and a lending library at this hospitable b&b.

Carriage House

1322 Catalina Street, Laguna Beach, CA 92651
Phone: (714) 494-8945
Key: Inn; 6 units; Moderate-Exp.; Smoking OK; Children OK; No credit cards

This Colonial inn in the artistic community of Laguna offers an array of room decors ranging from English and French country to a tropical, oriental theme. All guest quarters host large sitting rooms; and four of the rooms contain complete kitchens. Guest-room French doors open onto a courtyard and fountain, where guests may enjoy the family-style breakfast. Guests are welcomed with a bottle of wine and fresh fruit in the suite.

Casa Laguna Inn

2510 South Coast Highway, Laguna Beach, CA 92651
Phone: (714) 494-2996/(800) 233-0449 (CA)
Key: Inn/Hotel/Cottage; 20 units; Expensive-Del.; Smoking OK; Children OK; Credit cards

This hillside California Mission–Spanish Revival inn with secluded gardens and meandering paths offers flower-filled patios with spectacular ocean views. Guests also enjoy the grounds' shady terrace, a tropical-bird aviary, a courtyard, heated pool, and views from the bell tower at the restored 1930s villa that boasts hand-painted tile work and wrought-iron touches. The interior of the inn offers guests a library for relaxation and a pleasant mixture of contemporary and antique furnishings. The overnight accommodations include one private cottage, four suites, and fifteen guest rooms. All facilities offer private baths, individual decor, color cable television, and clock radios; many boast refrigerators, patios or balconies, and telephones. The inn serves a generous continental breakfast and afternoon refreshments of wine, hors d'oeuvres, teas, pâtés, cheeses, crackers, nuts, and gourmet snacks. The complimentary repasts are served in the library and may be enjoyed there, by the pool, or in the garden. Special events at the inn might include holiday boutiques, guitar music by the pool, and artistic displays.

Eiler's Inn

741 South Coast Highway, Laguna Beach, CA 92651
Phone: (714) 494-3004
Key: Inn/Hotel; 12 units; Expensive-Del.; Smoking OK; No children under 9; Credit cards

Located steps from the ocean in the heart of Laguna Beach is this European-style inn with French windows, lace curtains, and a courtyard with fountain, fish pond, and gardens. The guest rooms, built around the lush courtyard, are individually furnished in antiques and have private baths. One suite offers a kitchen, fireplace, and spectacular ocean view. Guests enjoy a library and living room downstairs as well as an ocean-view sun deck upstairs. The generous continental breakfast is served in the courtyard, as are evening wine and cheese. A classical guitarist is featured during the social period on weekends. Complimentary champagne, fresh flowers, and fruit baskets are placed in each guest room, and sun tea and coffee are available all day.

Home of Dennis & Karen Chernekoff

145 Cress Street, Laguna Beach, CA 92651
Phone: (714) 494-5451
Key: Home; 1 unit; Moderate; Limited smoking; No children; No credit cards

This home b&b offers just one intimate guest room with bath to guests who enjoy views of the sparkling Pacific, Catalina Island, and sunsets. A pretty beach and cove are easily reached just below the house via some private steps. The guest accommodation is furnished in antiques featuring a marble-topped dresser set. A king-size bed, private patio, and refrigerator make the guest room convenient and comfortable. The complimentary morning meal, served on the patio or at the dining-room table along with the morning newspaper, includes such delicacies as Belgian waffles and freshly baked pastries. Guests have use of the antique-furnished living room with TV; the innkeepers are able to provide "Pageant of the Masters" tickets during that popular summer festival.

Hotel San Maarten

696 South Coast Highway, Laguna Beach, CA 92651
Phone: (714) 494-9436/(800) 228-5691 (CA)/(800) 772-2539
Key: Inn/Hotel; 54 units; Moderate-Exp.; Smoking OK; Children
OK; Credit cards

The hotel creates a tropical setting with a courtyard, balconies, and abundant hanging plants. Guest rooms at the hotel are individually furnished in antiques; and suites offer their own Jacuzzis. A sauna, pool, and fine restaurant are located on the premises for all guests. The complimentary continental breakfast is served Monday through Friday only.

Casa Hermosa, Capistrano Beach

Casa Hermosa

34532 Camino Capistrano, P.O. Box 2761, Capistrano Beach, CA 92624
Phone: (714) 661-0637
Key: Home; 3 units; Moderate; Limited smoking; Children OK;
No credit cards

The 1929 Spanish-estate home is located on a bluff overlooking Dana Point and is within a short drive of the beach, marina, and shops. The guest rooms, with private baths, all host views of either the ocean, courtyard, or backyard swimming pool, which is available to guests. A full breakfast featuring scones, fresh fruit, and the chef's special of the day is offered in the dining room or the courtyard. Advance reservations are required.

Country Bay Inn

34862 Pacific Coast Highway, Capistrano Beach, CA 92624
Phone: (714) 496-6656
Key: Inn/Hotel; 28 units; Moderate-Exp.; Smoking OK; Children OK; Credit cards

Ocean views, wood-burning fireplaces, and private patios accent the antique-furnished rooms in this 1930s inn. All guest rooms contain wet bar, refrigerator, television, telephone, and sherry. A complimentary breakfast of croissants, juice, and coffee is served each morning. Free pickup from Amtrak is available.

Casa Tropicana B&B Inn

610 Avenida Victoria, San Clemente, CA 92672
Phone: (714) 492-1234
Key: Inn; 8 units; Deluxe; Limited smoking; Children OK; Credit cards

This carefully restored Spanish-style inn across from the beach and pier offers eight deluxe b&b accommodations on the second and third floors. The first floor of the building contains small retail shops. The deluxe rooms all feature fireplaces, color television, wet bars, and Jacuzzi tubs; some boast saunas. Guests enjoy a full complimentary breakfast chosen from an extensive menu of Spanish and American food in the tropical-style dining room. Decks located on guest-room floors offer panoramic views of the ocean.

Gull House

344 Whittley Avenue, P.O. Box 1381, Avalon, CA 90704
Phone: (213) 510-2547
Key: Home; 2 units; Moderate-Exp.; Smoking OK; No children; No credit cards

Located on beautiful Santa Catalina island just forty-five miles from Los Angeles, this bed & breakfast offers two complete suites with a rear-yard pool, spa, and adjoining barbecue area. The contemporary suites contain a spacious living room with fireplace, a bedroom, full bath, and "morning room" with table, chairs, and refrigerator. A continental breakfast is served each morning on the patio. The b&b closes in January and February.

The Inn on Mt. Ada, Avalon

The Inn on Mt. Ada

P.O. Box 2560, 207 Wrigley Road, Avalon, CA 90704
Phone: (213) 510-2030
Key: Inn; 6 units; Expensive-Del.; No smoking; No children under 14; Credit cards

The inn was built in 1921 as a summer home for the philanthropic owner of the island; in 1978 the home was given to the University of Southern California, which now leases the house for the purpose of maintaining a high-quality lodging establishment on the island. Located on five and one-half acres atop Mt. Ada, the old Georgian-Colonial house with shutters, moldings, and trim in grays, whites, and greens is surrounded by native trees and gardens and grants awesome views of the ocean. A traditionally furnished den, card lounge, and sunroom form the west wing of the first floor, while a spacious living room with vistas and an exquisite dining room make up the remaining common areas. The second floor of the mansion offers the four guest rooms and two suites of the inn. Such details as fireplaced sitting areas, walk-in closets, full bathrooms, and eclectic decor are found in these special accommodations. A full and hearty breakfast is included in the stay; lunches and dinners are offered as well.

Hotel Nipton

P.O. Box 357, 72 Nipton Road, Nipton, CA 92364
Phone: (619) 856-2335
Key: Inn; 4 units; Inexpensive; Smoking OK; Children OK; Credit cards

This restored turn-of-the-century hotel is a part of the small desert town of Nipton, a former 1885 gold-mining camp. The community (population: 30) in the East Mojave National Scenic Area is also owned by the b&b innkeepers, who purchased the town for restoration in 1986. The carefully renovated hotel maintains the early 1900s desert flavor with foot-thick adobe walls, lobby with wood-burning stove, and historic photos of the town's earlier days. Guests are treated to panoramic views of the desert and mountains from the hotel's front porch surrounded by rock and cactus gardens. The four guest rooms, which share baths, are named after prominent individuals from the hotel's past; Room #3 is named after Clara Bow, who stayed in the 1930s. Modern conveniences at the inn include central air and heating and a Jacuzzi for star gazing. A small café next door serves the inn's guests a full, hot, complimentary breakfast; guests help themselves to apricot brandy anytime.

Storybook Inn

28717 Highway 18, P.O. Box 362, Skyforest, CA 92385
Phone: (714) 336-1483
Key: Inn/Cottage; 10 units; Moderate-Exp.; No smoking; No children; Credit cards

This 9,000-square-foot, three-story mansion was built in the 1940s as an entertainment home. Located two miles from Lake Arrowhead, the inn has views for one-hundred miles. Accommodations include nine rooms decorated in antiques in the mansion, plus an adjoining two-bedroom cabin with fireplace and full kitchen. A breakfast of homemade muffins, a hot egg dish, fruit, and juice is served in the room, the dining area, or the solarium. The 2,500-square-foot lobby features plush carpeting, two massive brick fireplaces, and mahogany paneling. A conference room with wet bar and antiques is also available.

Bluebelle House, Lake Arrowhead

Bluebelle House

P.O. Box 2177, 263 S. State Highway 173, Lake Arrowhead, CA 92352
Phone: (714) 336-3292
Key: Inn; 5 units; Moderate; No smoking; No children under 11; Credit cards

A considerable amount of remodeling went into making this ship captain's home a bed & breakfast inn. The Alpine-style inn is just two-tenths of a mile from Lake Arrowhead Village and nearby private beaches that guests may enjoy. The parlor is soft blue hues is filled with cozy furnishings and a big rock fireplace. Guests also relax on the deck and hammock and may play darts or horseshoes. Three of the five guest rooms are on the main floor and share a bath; the "Edelweiss" room is the largest accommodation and boasts a private bath and special features. The two remaining rooms are upstairs and have private baths. The individually decorated rooms with queen-size beds, pretty sheets, and candy have varying themes, such as the Austrian-style "Edelweiss." Breakfast is on the tree-shaded deck or in the dining room and is served with fine linen, silver, and crystal.

Gold Mountain Manor

P.O. Box 2027, 1117 Anita, Big Bear City, CA 92314
Phone: (714) 585-6997
Key: Inn; 7 units; Moderate-Del.; No smoking; No children under 13; No credit cards

This beautiful, 7,000-square-foot mansion with bird's-eye-maple floors and beamed ceilings was built in the 1920s as a weekend lodge for wealthy gold miners. In the 1940s the lodge turned into a popular bordello. Now the log inn on two acres of pine trees has been meticulously restored and offers guests seven unique accommodations, six with fireplaces, one with a Jacuzzi, and two with private access to the veranda, a pool table, and a player piano. The guest rooms include three with private baths and range from a rustic decor with stone-hearth fireplace and pine floors to the "Clark Gable" room with an antique French walnut bed and the fireplace that honeymooned with Gable and Lombard. A homemade breakfast with such delights as crab quiche and baked cinnamon apples is served on the veranda or in the dining room; afternoon wine and hors d'oeuvres also are offered. The inn is one-half block from the National Forest.

Christmas House Bed & Breakfast Inn

9240 Archibald Avenue, Rancho Cucamonga, CA 91730
Phone: (714) 980-6450
Key: Inn; 5 units; Inexpensive-Mod.; No smoking; No children; No credit cards

Turn-of-the-century, gala, yuletide gatherings amidst intricate wood carvings and a profusion of red- and green-stained-glass

Christmas House Bed & Breakfast Inn, Rancho Cucamonga

windows inspired the name of this perfectly restored Queen Anne–Victorian that stands as a historical landmark. The interior of the house boasts period furnishings, seven fireplaces, and rich redwood and mahogany throughout; guests are welcome to enjoy the entire house. Guests also enjoy a sweeping veranda and one-half acre of gardens. The guest rooms are uniquely decorated in antiques and include shared and private baths, each outfitted with thick terry robes. The inn serves a generous continental breakfast weekdays and a full fare on weekends; the meal is served elegantly with antique china, white linens, and crystal. Arriving guests at the inn are greeted with a glass of local wine and sherry, and the innkeepers turn back beds and leave chocolate-truffle treats each evening. During the month of December, the house is decorated extravagantly in Victorian Christmas splendor, and the old-fashioned festivities include caroling, a wassail bowl, and figgy pudding. The holiday culminates with a New Year's murder-mystery gala in black-tie dress.

Wilkum Inn

P.O. Box 1115, 26770 Highway 243, Idyllwild, CA 92349
Phone: (714) 659-4087
Key: Inn; 5 units; Moderate; No smoking; No children; No credit cards

This two-story, shingled mountain retreat built around 1938 is situated on three-quarters acre of lilacs, pines, and oaks. The nicely restored home's interiors boast warm knotty-pine paneling and Pennsylvania Dutch accents. A common room provides a large stone fireplace; guests breakfast in the dining room over-looking the patio. The five guest rooms are individually decorated with antiques, lace curtains, and collectibles. The three upstairs rooms share a bath but boast in-room sinks; the downstairs "Garden Room" offers a private bath and French doors opening onto the yard. The inn also offers "The Loft," a fully equipped private unit with kitchen and living room but none of the b&b amenities. Guests enjoy a gourmet continental breakfast that includes four juices, fruit compote, and homemade breads, muffins, *abelskivers*, or Belgian waffles. Wines and self-serve beverages are available all day, and popcorn or cheese and crackers are set out each evening.

Villa Royale Bed & Breakfast Inn

1620 Indian Trail, Palm Springs, CA 92264
Phone: (619) 327-2314
Key: Inn; 31 units; Moderate-Del.; Smoking OK; No children; Credit cards

This "international" country inn on three and one-half land-scaped acres with wandering brick paths, streams, and gardens offers a unique b&b escape to those wanting a taste of European elegance. Each of the thirty-one suites and guest rooms is deco-rated uniquely in antique furnishings, colors, and art imported and selected personally by the gracious innkeepers from a differ-ent European country, along with such special handicraft touches as custom-designed quilts, woven hangings, carvings, sculptures, and pillows. The deluxe accommodations boast fully equipped kitchens or refrigerators, phones, color cable television carefully concealed, oversized beds, many wood-burning fireplaces, coordi-nated wall coverings, and private patios landscaped with plants from the "theme" country; a few units boast private spas. The units are grouped around three gracious courtyards framed by bougainvillea and shade trees. Guests enjoy the tranquil "classical music" courtyard, an outdoor living room with fireplace, two swimming pools, a Jacuzzi, a roof-top sun deck, barbecues, and bicycles. The breakfast of fresh juice, fruit, and home-baked muf-fins is served each morning on the arched poolside patio or on the sun patio; the morning newspaper is left at each door. Gourmet international lunches and dinners are offered; a bar is open to guests.

Halbig's Hacienda

432 South Citrus Avenue, Escondido, CA 92027
Phone: (619) 745-1296
Key: Home; 3 units; Inexpensive; Smoking OK; Children OK; No credit cards

Nestled among fruit trees and gardens, with views of surrounding mountains, this adobe ranch–style home offers country atmosphere with proximity to restaurants, stores, the San Diego Wild Animal Park, and other north-county attractions. Three guest rooms with several antiques and shared baths are available to guests. Guests enjoy a television, a long veranda, and discounts for extended stays. Pets and children are welcome.

Rock Haus

410 15th Street, Del Mar, CA 92014
Phone: (619) 481-3764
Key: Inn; 10 units; Moderate-Exp.; No smoking; No children; Credit cards

The Early California bungalow-style house is situated in the heart of Del Mar Village, yet it boasts ocean views. Most of the ten guest rooms offer ocean views, and all have individual decor, with private- and shared-bath accommodations. The "Huntsman's Room" features a fireplace. Guests enjoy a continental fare each morning consisting of fresh fruit, muffins, breads, and juices and late-afternoon wine and cheese served in the cozy living room. Shops, restaurants, and the beach are a stroll away, and innkeepers provide courtesy pickup service from Amtrak three blocks away.

The Bed & Breakfast Inn at La Jolla

7753 Draper Avenue, La Jolla, CA 92037
Phone: (619) 456-2066
Key: Inn; 16 units; Moderate-Del.; Limited smoking; No children under 12; Credit cards

This 1913 Irving Gill–built b&b is a part of the San Diego Historical Registry and was the John Philip Sousa family residence for several years in the 1920s. Cubist-style architecture describes the exterior of the inn, which is surrounded by the original gardens. The main house contains ten of the guest rooms; six are located in the annex. Guest rooms at the inn are elegantly and individually decorated in Laura Ashley or Ralph Lauren fabrics, and each room has either a queen-size bed or two twins. Fresh fruit, sherry, and flowers add a nice touch to each guest room. A light breakfast is served on fine china and linen on a tray in the room or in the garden, or the guest may join with others in the dining room. This b&b is located in the heart of La Jolla's cultural complex, just one and one-half blocks from the beach.

Cedar Creek Inn

P.O. Box 1466, Alpine, CA 92001
8020 Highway 79, Descanso, CA 92001
Phone: (619) 445-9605
Key: Home; 3 units; Inexpensive; Limited smoking; Children OK; No credit cards

Part of the sprawling, historic Ellis Ranch on Sweetwater River, this mountain-cottage retreat is surrounded by three and three-quarters acres of trees and lawn. The single-story house offers guests patios and an exercise pool in its private, country setting forty-five minutes from San Diego. The three guest accommodations include the "Cedar Creek Suite," a private studio apartment with deck, kitchen, and bath, as well as two guest rooms with private sitting areas that share a kitchen and bath. Rolls, coffee, and orange juice are served each morning in the kitchen of each unit at this reasonable b&b.

Shackelford Guest Home

11532 Rolling Hills Drive, El Cajon, CA 92020
Phone: (619) 442-3164
Key: Home; 3 units; Moderate; No smoking; Children OK; No credit cards

The artist-innkeeper of this b&b designed and built the home in an exclusive San Diego suburb. The unique interiors feature high-beamed ceilings, picture windows that take advantage of the beautiful mountain and hill views, and sliding glass doors that lead to shaded patios. Guests enjoy spacious rooms (with additional beds available), television, telephone, and private entrance; children are welcomed here with a nursery room and outdoor play areas. A full breakfast is served graciously and features juice from the b&b's own hand picked oranges. Golf- and tennis-club privileges are extended to guests.

Britt House, San Diego

Britt House

406 Maple, San Diego, CA 92103
Phone: (619) 234-2926
Key: Inn/Cottage; 10 units; Moderate-Exp.; No smoking; Children OK; Credit cards

This carefully restored Queen Anne–Victorian is a pleasant mixture of period furnishings, collectibles, and cozy touches such as stuffed animals and in-room cookies and fruit. Claw-foot tubs grace one of the shared baths. The separate cottage contains a kitchen. Daily homemade yeast breads and egg dishes are a part of the full breakfast. A formal afternoon tea with Irish tea and a variety of sweet and hearty delectables is served in the parlor with its twelve-foot-high ceilings, oak-mantel fireplace, elaborate fretwork, and two-story stained-glass windows.

The Cottage

P.O. Box 3292, San Diego, CA 92103
Phone: (619) 299-1564
Key: Cottage; 1 unit; Inexpensive-Mod.; Limited smoking; No children; Credit cards

Located in an older residential and rural canyon area of the city, this Victorian-furnished guest house has a full kitchen, full bath, wood-burning stove, and oak pump organ. A freshly baked continental breakfast is served each morning.

Edgemont Inn

1955 Edgemont Street, San Diego, CA 92102
Phone: (619) 238-1677/(800) 822-1955 (CA)
Key: Inn; 4 units; Moderate-Exp.; No smoking; No children; No credit cards

This country-style b&b is right in the heart of the city and close to all tourist attractions. Guest rooms are decorated individually in antiques, lace, and teddy bears. Hosts serve evening refreshments in the parlor, and the full breakfast, presented on fine china and silver, can be enjoyed in the room (for special occasions only), the dining room, or the newly restored lattice greenhouse.

Heritage Park Bed & Breakfast Inn, San Diego

Heritage Park Bed & Breakfast Inn

2470 Heritage Park Row, San Diego, CA 92110
Phone: (619) 295-7088
Key: Inn; 9 units; Moderate-Exp.; No smoking; No children under 14; Credit cards

This Queen Anne–Victorian home with a two-story corner tower and encircling veranda sits on San Diego's historical park in the company of other classic structures and fronted by cobblestone walkways. Totally restored to its original floor plan, this inn offers vintage movies each evening in the antique-filled parlor. Accommodations with private and shared baths are uniquely decorated in period antiques and have Victorian wall coverings or stenciling, polished wooden floors, oriental rugs, and handmade quilts. All of the antiques at the inn are for sale. A full gourmet breakfast, featuring the inn's award-winning sweet bread and complete with roses and Depression glassware, may be enjoyed in bed, in the room, or on the sunny veranda. A special five-course candlelight dinner may be arranged in advance. Special packages are available; Christmas candlelight tours are offered nightly the entire month of December.

Keating House Inn

2331 Second Avenue, San Diego, CA 92101
Phone: (619) 239-8585
Key: Inn; 4 units; Moderate; Limited smoking; No children under 12; Credit cards

This historic 1888-built Queen Anne–Victorian landmark on Bankers Hill overlooks the bay just four blocks from the Balboa Park attractions. Pleasant, sunny gardens and shaded patios provide relaxation around the restored home with stained-glass windows, two-story bay windows, gabled roofs, and tower. The four upstairs guest rooms, comfortably decorated in country antiques and plants, share two baths; two rooms share a balcony. Guests may enjoy two parlors and a music room with grand piano. The second parlor is the site of the morning breakfast of fresh fruit compote, freshly baked breads, assorted rolls, and juice. Extras at the inn include evening sherry and wine, bed turn-down service with chocolate truffles on the pillows, and antique kimonos in the baths.

Surf Manor and Cottages

P.O. Box 7695, San Diego, CA 92107
Phone: (619) 225-9765
Key: Cottages; 7 units; Moderate-Exp.; Limited smoking; Children OK; No credit cards

This "two part" b&b offering, available September through June, consists of "Surf Manor," directly on the oceanfront with wide, sandy beach and near the Ocean Beach Fishing Pier, and "The Cottages," consisting of four original beach cottages within a block of South Mission Beach and boasting a small private garden. Each cozy three- or four-room suite, decorated in assorted antiques and country-spring wallpapers and fabrics, boasts privacy with its own living room, bedroom, bath, kitchen, color television, and parking place. Each refrigerator is stocked with the ingredients for a continental or full English breakfast as requested. The units are self-catered the remainder of the year on weekly or monthly rates.

Julian Hotel

P.O. Box 856, 2032 Main Street, Julian, CA 92036
Phone: (619) 765-0201
Key: Inn/Hotel/Cottage; 17 units; Inexpensive-Mod.; Smoking OK; No children under 13 (weekends)/Children OK (weeknights); Credit cards

The only hotel survivor of the area's mining-boom days, the hotel was constructed by freed slaves in 1897 and is listed in the National Register of Historic Places. The inn is completely furnished in authentic American antiques from the turn of the century (including some original hotel pieces such as the upright piano), and the lobby and some of the guest rooms have ceilings of both pressed tin and redwood car siding. Guest rooms have Victorian wallpapers, headboard canopies, and cozy comforters or quilts. The "Honeymoon House" is a one-bedroom cottage with woodburning stove and lots of romantic lace. The complimentary full breakfast of eggs Florentine, fruit, nut bread, homemade granola, and juice is served in the dining room or on the native-stone patios surrounded by colorful flowers.

Pine Hills Lodge

2960 La Posada Way, Julian, CA 92036
Phone: (619) 765-1100
Key: Inn/Hotel/Cottages; 17 units; Inexpensive-Exp.; Smoking OK; Children OK; Credit cards

The rustic, wooden lodge built in 1912 features a giant native-stone fireplace in the lobby, a country-style dining room, and an authentic western bar. The guest accommodations include European-style rooms in the lodge with wash basins and claw-foot tubs down the hall and a dozen cottages, some with fireplaces and patios. A continental breakfast is served to guests every day except Sunday. A barbecue dinner–theater is offered on weekends.

Shadow Mountain Ranch

2771 Frisius Road, Box 791, Julian, CA 92036
Phone: (619) 765-0323
Key: Home; 6 units; Moderate; No smoking; No children; No credit cards

This ranch-style b&b was once an apple orchard and cattle ranch and is surrounded by meadows and pine-covered mountains. The individually decorated guest rooms include such features as wood-burning stoves, antiques, and Indian artifacts. One unusual guest accommodation is actually an "adult" tree house nestled in a century-old oak. Besides the full ranch breakfast, guests may enjoy hot tub, hiking trails, or even the feeding of ranch animals. The evening brings a fireside glass of sherry or cup of warm vanilla milk. Guests also enjoy a lap pool, horseshoes, and badminton.

Brookside Farm Bed & Breakfast Inn

1373 Marron Valley Road, Dulzura, CA 92017
Phone: (619) 468-3043
Key: Inn/Cottage; 8 units; Inexpensive-Mod.; Limited smoking; No children; No credit cards

This peaceful farmhouse with cottage boasts a year-round stream, gigantic old oak trees, a European-style barn, a large garden, vineyard, and fruit trees, along with all the goats, chickens, and geese you would expect to find in this setting. Each of the guests may enjoy a hot tub, hiking trails, or even the feeding of ranch animals. The evening brings a fireside glass of sherry or cup rugs. The "Attic" is filled with grandma's mementos, while the "Summer Kitchen" is decorated in cooking memorabilia. All guest accommodations in the farmhouse share baths. This farm b&b doesn't disappoint at breakfast time, when all guests gather at 9:00 A.M. for farm-fresh omelettes and egg dishes, fruits, juices, and jams as well as homemade breads, muffins, and biscuits. The breakfast and gourmet dinners (offered on weekends and holidays for $15 per person) are prepared by the innkeeper/chef, Edd, who also offers a cooking school one weekend each month. The terraces and garden at this farm b&b are available for small weddings.

Referral Agencies and B&B Associations in California

A majority of the following referral agencies and associations request that a self-addressed, stamped envelope accompany any requests for information.

Referral Agencies:

Accommodation Referral
Reservations
P.O. Box 59
St. Helena, CA 94574
(707) 963-8466/944-8891
Serving: Napa County

Accommodations in Santa
Barbara
1216 State Street
Santa Barbara, CA 93101
(805) 963-9518
Serving: Santa Barbara

American Family Inn/Bed &
Breakfast
San Francisco
P.O. Box 349
San Francisco, CA 94101
(415) 931-3083
*Serving: San Francisco,
Carmel/Monterey, Marin
County, Wine Country, and
Los Angeles*

American Historic Homes Bed
& Breakfast
P.O. Box 336
Dana Point, CA 92629
(714) 496-6953
*Serving: California, United
States*

Bed & Breakfast Exchange
1458 Lincoln Avenue #3
Calistoga, CA 94515
(707) 942-5900
*Serving: Napa and Sonoma
counties, Gold Country, San
Francisco, northern coast*

Bed & Breakfast Homestay
P.O. Box 326
Cambria, CA 93428
(805) 927-4613/(800) 447-6667
(CA)
*Serving: region from Monterey
to Santa Barbara*

Bed & Breakfast International
151 Ardmore Road
Kensington, CA 94707
(415) 525-4569
*Serving: California, selected
U. S. cities*

Bed & Breakfast of Los
Angeles
32074 Waterside Lane
Westlake, CA 91361
(818) 889-8870/889-7325
*Serving: Ventura, Los Angeles,
and Orange counties and
the limited coast from San
Diego to San Francisco*

California Houseguests
International
18653 Ventura Blvd. #190B
Tarzana, CA 91356
(818) 344-7878
Serving: California

Carolyn's Bed & Breakfast
Homes in San Diego
416 Third Ave. #25
Chula Vista, CA 92010
(619) 422-7009
*Serving: San Diego County,
Los Angeles area*

Christian B&B of America
P.O. Box 336
Dana Point, CA 92629
(714) 496-6953
*Serving: California, United
States*

Country Inns Lodging
Information
(707) 964-7682
Serving: Mendocino coast

D.B. Tourist
Company-Reservation
Service
1806 Pampas Avenue
Santa Barbara, CA 93101
(805) 687-8605
*Serving: Santa Barbara,
Ventura, Camarillo, Santa
Maria, and Morro Bay*

Digs West
8191 Crowley Circle
Buena Park, CA 90621
(714) 739-1669
*Serving: Santa Barbara to San
Diego; California*

El Camino Real Bed &
Breakfast
P.O. Box 7155
Northridge, CA 91327-7155
(818) 363-6753
Serving: southern California

Eye Openers Bed & Breakfast
Reservations
P.O. Box 694
Altadena, CA 91001
(213) 684-4428/(818) 797-2055
Serving: California

Hospitality Plus
P.O. Box 388
San Juan Capistrano, CA
92693
(714) 496-7050
Serving: California

Inns of Point Reyes
P.O. Box 145
Inverness, CA 94937
(415) 663-1420
Serving: west Marin County

Laguna Beach B&B
33261 Mesa Vista
Dana Point, CA 92629
(714) 496-7050
*Serving: Laguna Beach,
Newport Beach, San
Clemente*

Megan's Friends Bed &
Breakfast Reservations
1776 Royal Way
San Luis Obispo, CA 93401
(805) 544-4406
*Serving: San Luis Obispo and
Santa Barbara counties and
U. S. referrals*

Rent A Room Bed & Breakfast
11531 Varna Street
Garden Grove, CA 92640
(714) 638-1406
*Serving: region from Los
Angeles to San Diego*

Wine Country Bed &
Breakfast
P.O. Box 3211

Santa Rosa, CA 95403
(707) 578-1661
*Serving: Wine Country,
northern California*

Wine Country Reservations
P.O. Box 5059
Napa, CA 94581-0059
(707) 257-7757/944-1222
Serving: Napa Valley

Associations

Bed & Breakfast Association
of Napa Valley
P.O. Box 5059
Napa, CA 94581-0059
(707) 257-7757
Serving: Napa Valley

Bed & Breakfast Innkeepers
Guild of Santa Barbara
P.O. Box 20246
Santa Barbara, CA 93120
Serving: Santa Barbara

Bed & Breakfast Innkeepers of
Humboldt County
P.O. Box KS-40
Ferndale, CA 95536
(707) 786-4000
Serving: Humboldt County

Bed & Breakfast Innkeepers of
Santa Cruz
P.O. Box 464
Santa Cruz, CA 95061
(408) 425-8212
Serving: Santa Cruz County

Bed & Breakfast Innkeepers of
Southern California
P.O. Box 15425
Los Angeles, CA 90015
*Serving: region from Cambria
to San Diego*

Bed & Breakfast Inns of Gold
Country
P.O. Box 462
Sonora, CA 95370
(916) 626-6136
*Serving: Highway 49 from
Downieville to Mariposa*

Monterey Peninsula Bed &
Breakfast
598 Laine Street
Monterey, CA 93940
(408) 372-4777
*Serving: Monterey, Pacific
Grove*

Sacramento Innkeepers'
Association
2209 Capitol Avenue
Sacramento, CA 95816
(916) 441-3214
Serving: Sacramento

Wine Country Inns of Sonoma
County
P.O. Box 51
Geyserville, CA 95441
(707) 443-INNS
*Serving: Sonoma County
Wine Country*

Yosemite Bed & Breakfasts of
Mariposa County
P.O. Box 1100
Mariposa, CA 95338
*Serving: Yosemite Park,
Mariposa County (Gold
Country)*

INDEX

260

Other fine books from Globe Pequot on the California area

Guide to the Country Inns of the West Coast
Getaway Guide I & II
Parks of the Pacific Coast
Photographing the North American West
Walking from Inn to Inn: San Francisco Bay Area

Other B&B books from Globe Pequot

Bed & Breakfast in the Caribbean
Bed & Breakfast in the Mid-Atlantic States
Bed & Breakfast in New England
The Bed & Breakfast Traveler: Touring the West Coast
Best Bed & Breakfast in the World
How to Open & Operate a B&B Home